I0448436

Informing the legislative debate since 1914

Preserving Homeownership:
Foreclosure Prevention Initiatives

Katie Jones
Analyst in Housing Policy

November 20, 2013

Congressional Research Service

7-5700

www.crs.gov

R40210

Summary

The foreclosure rate in the United States began to rise rapidly beginning around the middle of 2006 and has remained elevated ever since. Losing a home to foreclosure can hurt homeowners in many ways; for example, homeowners who have been through a foreclosure may have difficulty finding a new place to live or obtaining a loan in the future. Furthermore, concentrated foreclosures can drag down nearby home prices, and large numbers of abandoned properties can negatively affect communities. Finally, elevated levels of foreclosures can destabilize the housing market, which can in turn negatively impact the economy as a whole.

There is a broad consensus that there are many negative consequences associated with rising foreclosure rates. Since the foreclosure rate began to rise, Congress and both the Bush and Obama Administrations have initiated efforts aimed at preventing further increases in foreclosures and helping more families preserve homeownership. These efforts currently include the Making Home Affordable program, which includes both the Home Affordable Refinance Program (HARP) and the Home Affordable Modification Program (HAMP); the Hardest Hit Fund; the Federal Housing Administration (FHA) Short Refinance Program; and the National Foreclosure Mitigation Counseling Program (NFMCP), which provides funding for counseling for homeowners facing foreclosure and is administered by NeighborWorks America. Two other initiatives, Hope for Homeowners and the Emergency Homeowners Loan Program (EHLP), expired at the end of FY2011.

While there is a broad consensus that there are many negative consequences related to foreclosures, there is less consensus over whether the federal government should have a role in preventing foreclosures and, if so, what that role should be. Furthermore, many existing federal foreclosure prevention initiatives have been criticized as being ineffective. This has led some policymakers to suggest that changes should be made to these initiatives to try to make them more effective, while other policymakers have argued that some of these initiatives should be eliminated entirely. In the 112th Congress, the House of Representatives passed a series of bills that, if enacted, would have terminated several foreclosure prevention initiatives. However, these bills were not considered by the Senate.

While many observers agree that slowing the pace of foreclosures is an important policy goal, there are several challenges associated with designing foreclosure prevention initiatives. These challenges include implementation issues, such as deciding who has the authority to make mortgage modifications, developing the capacity to complete widespread modifications, and assessing the possibility that homeowners with modified loans will default again in the future. Other challenges are related to the perception of unfairness in providing help to one set of homeowners over others, the problem of inadvertently providing incentives for borrowers to default, and the possibility of setting an unwanted precedent for future mortgage lending.

Contents

Figures

Tables

Appendixes

Contacts

Introduction and Background

The foreclosure rate in the United States began to rise rapidly around the middle of 2006, and has remained elevated since that time. The large increase in home foreclosures has negatively impacted individual households, local communities, and the economy as a whole. Consequently, an issue before Congress has been whether to use federal resources and authority to help prevent some home foreclosures and, if so, how to best accomplish this objective. This report provides background on the increase in foreclosure rates in recent years. It also describes recent attempts to preserve homeownership that have been implemented by the federal government, and briefly outlines current proposals for further foreclosure prevention activities. It concludes with a discussion of some of the challenges inherent in designing foreclosure prevention initiatives.

Foreclosure refers to formal legal proceedings initiated by a mortgage lender against a homeowner after the homeowner has missed a certain number of payments on his or her mortgage.[1] When a foreclosure is completed, the homeowner loses his or her home, which is either repossessed by the lender or sold at auction to repay the outstanding debt. In general, the term "foreclosure" can refer to the foreclosure process or the completion of a foreclosure. This report deals primarily with preventing foreclosure completions.

In order for the foreclosure process to begin, two things must happen: a homeowner must fail to make a certain number of payments on his or her mortgage, and a lender must decide to initiate foreclosure proceedings rather than pursue other options (such as offering a repayment plan or a loan modification). A borrower that misses one or more payments is usually referred to as being delinquent on a loan; when a borrower has missed three or more payments, he or she is generally considered to be in default. Lenders can choose to begin foreclosure proceedings after a homeowner defaults on his or her mortgage, although lenders vary in how quickly they begin foreclosure proceedings after a borrower goes into default. Furthermore, the rules governing foreclosures, and the length of time the process takes, vary by state.

Foreclosure Trends

Home prices rose rapidly throughout some regions of the United States beginning in 2001. Housing has traditionally been seen as a safe investment that can offer an opportunity for high returns, and rapidly rising home prices reinforced this view. During this housing "boom," many people decided to buy homes or take out second mortgages in order to access their increasing home equity. Furthermore, rising home prices and low interest rates contributed to a sharp increase in people refinancing their mortgages; for example, between 2000 and 2003, the number of refinanced mortgage loans jumped from 2.5 million to over 15 million.[2] Around the same time, subprime lending, which generally refers to making mortgage loans to individuals with credit scores that are too low to qualify for prime rate mortgages, also began to increase, reaching a peak between 2004 and 2006. However, beginning in 2006 and 2007, home sales started to

---

[1] For a more detailed discussion of the foreclosure process and the factors that contribute to a lender's decision to pursue foreclosure, see CRS Report RL34232, *The Process, Data, and Costs of Mortgage Foreclosure*, coordinated by Darryl E. Getter.

[2] U.S. Department of Housing and Urban Development, Office of Policy Development and Research, *An Analysis of Mortgage Refinancing, 2001-2003*, November 2004, p.1, http://www.huduser.org/Publications/pdf/MortgageRefinance03.pdf.

decline, home prices stopped rising and began to fall in many regions, and the rates of homeowners becoming delinquent on their mortgages or going into foreclosure began to increase.

The percentage of home loans in the foreclosure process in the U.S. began to rise rapidly beginning around the middle of 2006. Although not all homes in the foreclosure process will end in a foreclosure completion, an increase in the number of loans in the foreclosure process is generally accompanied by an increase in the number of homes on which a foreclosure is completed. According to the Mortgage Bankers Association, an industry group, about 1% of all home loans were in the foreclosure process in the second quarter of 2006. By the fourth quarter of 2009, the rate had more than quadrupled to over 4.5%, and it peaked in the fourth quarter of 2010 at about 4.6%. Since then, the percentage of mortgages in the foreclosure process has started to decrease, but still remains high compared to the early and mid-2000s. In the second quarter of 2013, the rate of loans in the foreclosure process was about 3.3%.

Figure 1 illustrates the trends in the rates of all mortgages, subprime mortgages, and prime mortgages in the foreclosure process over the past several years.

Figure 1. Percentage of Mortgages in the Foreclosure Process
Q1 2001 – Q2 2013

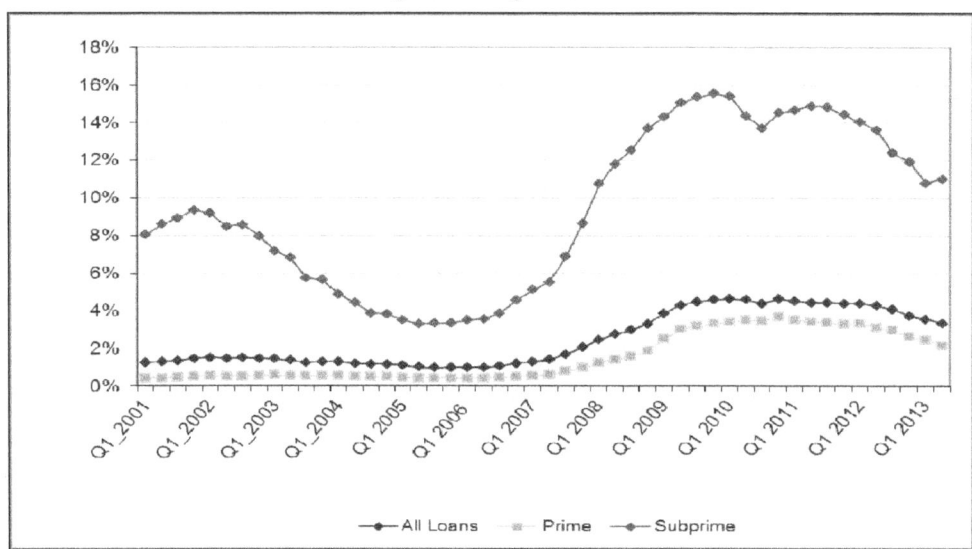

Source: Figure created by CRS using data from the Mortgage Bankers Association.

Notes: The Mortgage Bankers Association (MBA) is one of several organizations that reports delinquency and foreclosure data. MBA estimates that its data cover about 80% of outstanding first-lien mortgages on single family properties.

The foreclosure rate for subprime loans has always been higher than the foreclosure rate for prime loans. For example, in the second quarter of 2006, just over 3.5% of subprime loans were in the foreclosure process compared to less than 0.5% of prime loans. However, both prime and subprime loans have seen increases in foreclosure rates over the past several years. Like the foreclosure rate for all loans combined, the foreclosure rates for prime and subprime loans both more than quadrupled after 2006, with the rate of subprime loans in the foreclosure process increasing to over 15.5% in the fourth quarter of 2009 and the rate of prime loans in the foreclosure process increasing to more than 3% over the same time period. As of the second quarter of 2013, the rate of subprime loans in the foreclosure process was about 11%, while the rate of prime loans in the foreclosure process was about 2%.

In addition to mortgages that were in the foreclosure process, an additional 2.55% of all mortgages were 90 or more days delinquent but not yet in foreclosure in the second quarter of 2013. These are mortgages that are in default and generally could be in the foreclosure process, but for one reason or another the mortgage servicer has not started the foreclosure process yet. Such reasons could include the volume of delinquent loans that the servicer is dealing with, delays due to efforts to modify the mortgage before beginning foreclosure, or voluntary pauses in foreclosure activity put in place by the servicer. Considering mortgages that are 90 or more days delinquent, as well as mortgages that are actively in the foreclosure process, may give a more complete picture of the number of mortgages that are in danger of foreclosure.

Impacts of Foreclosure

Losing a home to foreclosure can have a number of negative effects on a household. For many families, losing a home can mean losing the household's largest store of wealth. Furthermore, foreclosure can negatively impact a borrower's creditworthiness, making it more difficult for him or her to buy a home in the future. Finally, losing a home to foreclosure can also mean that a household loses many of the less tangible benefits of owning a home. Research has shown that these benefits might include increased civic engagement that results from having a stake in the community, and better health, school, and behavioral outcomes for children.[3]

Some homeowners might have difficulty finding a place to live after losing their home to foreclosure. Many will become renters. However, some landlords may be unwilling to rent to families whose credit has been damaged by a foreclosure, limiting the options open to these families. There can also be spillover effects from foreclosures on current renters. Renters living in buildings facing foreclosure may be required to move, even if they are current on their rent payments. As more homeowners become renters and as more current renters are displaced when their landlords face foreclosure, pressure on local rental markets may increase, and more families may have difficulty finding affordable rental housing. Some observers have also raised the concern that a large increase in foreclosures could increase homelessness, either because families who lost their homes have trouble finding new places to live or because the increased demand for rental housing makes it more difficult for families to find adequate, affordable units.

If foreclosures are concentrated, they can also have negative impacts on communities. Many foreclosures in a single neighborhood may depress surrounding home values.[4] If foreclosed homes stand vacant for long periods of time, they can attract crime and blight, especially if they are not well-maintained. Concentrated foreclosures also place pressure on local governments,

---

[3] For example, see Donald R. Haurin, Toby L. Parcel, and R. Jean Haurin, *The Impact of Homeownership on Child Outcomes*, Joint Center for Housing Studies, Harvard University, Low-Income Homeownership Working Paper Series, October 2001, http://www.jchs harvard.edu/publications/homeownership/liho01-14.pdf, and Denise DiPasquale and Edward L. Glaeser, *Incentives and Social Capital: Are Homeowners Better Citizens?*, National Bureau of Economic Research, NBER Working Paper 6363, Cambridge, MA, January 1998, http://www nber.org/papers/w6363.pdf? new_window=1.

[4] For a review of the literature on the impact of foreclosures on nearby house prices, see Kai-yan Lee, *Foreclosure's Price-Depressing Spillover Effects on Local Properties:A Literature Review*, Federal Reserve Bank of Boston, Community Affairs Discussion Paper, No. 2008-01, September 2008, http://www.bos frb.org/commdev/pcadp/2008/pcadp0801.pdf.

which can lose property tax revenue and may have to step in to maintain vacant foreclosed properties.

The Policy Problem

There has been a broad bipartisan consensus that the rapid rise in foreclosures has had negative consequences on households and communities. For example, in 2008, Representative Spencer Bachus, then-chairman of the House Committee on Financial Services, said that "[i]t is in everyone's best interest as a general rule to prevent foreclosures. Foreclosures have a negative impact not only on families but also on their neighbors, their property value, and on the community and local government."[5] Former Senator Chris Dodd, during his tenure as chairman of the Senate Committee on Banking, Housing, and Urban Affairs, described an "overwhelming tide of foreclosures ravaging our neighborhoods and forcing thousands of American families from their homes."[6]

There is less agreement among policymakers about how much the federal government should do to prevent foreclosures. Proponents of enacting government policies and using government resources to prevent foreclosures argue that, in addition to being a compassionate response to the plight of individual homeowners, such action may prevent further damage to home values and communities that can be caused by concentrated foreclosures. Supporters also suggest that preventing foreclosures may help stabilize the economy as a whole. Opponents of government foreclosure prevention programs argue that foreclosure prevention should be worked out between lenders and borrowers without government interference. Opponents express concern that people who do not really need help, or who are not perceived to deserve help, could unfairly take advantage of government foreclosure prevention programs. They argue that taxpayers' money should not be used to help people who can still afford their loans but want to get more favorable mortgage terms, people who may be seeking to pass their losses on to the lender or the taxpayer, or people who knowingly took on mortgages that they could not afford.

Despite the concerns surrounding foreclosure prevention programs, and disagreement over the proper role of the government in preserving homeownership, Congress and the executive branch have both taken actions aimed at preventing foreclosures in recent years. Many private companies and state and local governments have also undertaken their own foreclosure prevention efforts, although these efforts are not the focus of this report.

Why Might a Household Find Itself Facing Foreclosure?

There are many reasons that a household might fall behind on its mortgage payments. Some borrowers may have simply taken out loans on homes that they could not afford. However, many homeowners who believed they were acting responsibly when they took out a mortgage nonetheless find themselves facing foreclosure. The reasons households might have difficulty

---

[5] Representative Spencer Bachus, "Remarks of Ranking Member Spencer Bachus During Full Committee Hearing on Loan Modifications," press release, November 12, 2008, http://bachus house.gov/index.php?option=com_content& task=view&id=160&Itemid=104.

[6] Senator Chris Dodd, "Dodd Statement on Government Loan Modification Program," statement, November 11, 2008, http://dodd.senate.gov/?q=node/4620.

making their mortgage payments include changes in personal circumstances, which can be exacerbated by macroeconomic conditions, and features of the mortgages themselves.

Changes in Household Circumstances

Changes in a household's circumstances can affect its ability to pay its mortgage. For example, a number of events can leave a household with a lower income than it anticipated when it bought its home. Such changes in circumstances can include a lost job, an illness, or a change in family structure due to divorce or death. Families that expected to maintain a certain level of income may struggle to make payments if a household member loses a job or faces a cut in pay, or if a two-earner household becomes a single-earner household. Unexpected medical bills or other unforeseen expenses can also make it difficult for a family to stay current on its mortgage.

Furthermore, sometimes a change in circumstances means that a home no longer meets a family's needs, and the household needs to sell the home. These changes can include having to relocate for a job or needing a bigger house to accommodate a new child or an aging parent. Traditionally, households that needed to move, or who experienced a decline in income, could usually sell their existing homes. However, the recent decline in home prices in many communities nationwide has left many homeowners "underwater," meaning that they owe more on their mortgages than the houses are worth.[7] This limits homeowners' ability to sell their homes for enough money to pay off their mortgages if they have to move; many of these families are effectively trapped in their current homes and mortgages because they cannot afford to sell their homes at a loss.

The risks presented by changing personal circumstances have always existed for anyone who took out a loan, but deteriorating macroeconomic conditions, such as falling home prices and increasing unemployment, have made families especially vulnerable to losing their homes for such reasons. The fall in home values that has left some homeowners owing more than the value of their homes makes it difficult for homeowners to sell their homes in order to avoid a foreclosure if they experience a change in circumstances, and it increases the incentive for homeowners to walk away from their homes if they can no longer afford their mortgage payments. Along with the fall in home values, another recent macroeconomic trend has been high unemployment. More households experiencing job loss and the resultant income loss have made it difficult for many families to keep up with their monthly mortgage payments.

Mortgage Features

Borrowers might also find themselves having difficulty staying current on their loan payments due in part to features of their mortgages. In previous years, there had been an increase in the use of alternative mortgage products whose terms differ significantly from the traditional 30-year, fixed interest rate mortgage model.[8] While borrowers with traditional mortgages are not immune

---

[7] Owing more on the mortgage than the home is worth is also known as having "negative equity" in the home. According to CoreLogic, a data research firm, nearly 11 million households, or about 22% of all properties with a mortgage, had negative equity in their homes as of the second quarter of 2012. See CoreLogic, "CoreLogic Reports Number of Residential Properties in Negative Equity Decreases Again in Second Quarter of 2012," press release, September 12, 2012, http://www.corelogic.com/about-us/researchtrends/asset_upload_file486_16724.pdf.

[8] For a fuller discussion of these types of mortgage products and their effects, see CRS Report RL33775, *Alternative Mortgages: Causes and Policy Implications of Troubled Mortgage Resets in the Subprime and Alt-A Markets*, by Edward V. Murphy.

to delinquency and foreclosure, many of these alternative mortgage features seem to have increased the risk that a homeowner will have trouble staying current on his or her mortgage. Many of these loans were structured to have low monthly payments in the early stages and then adjust to higher monthly payments depending on prevailing market interest rates and/or the length of time the borrower held the mortgage. Furthermore, many of these mortgage features made it more difficult for homeowners to quickly build equity in their homes. Some examples of the features of these alternative mortgage products are listed below.

Adjustable-Rate Mortgages

With an adjustable-rate mortgage (ARM), a borrower's interest rate can change at predetermined intervals, often based on changes in an index. The new interest rate can be higher or lower than the initial interest rate, and monthly payments can also be higher or lower based on both the new interest rate and any interest rate or payment caps.[9] Some ARMs also include an initial low interest rate known as a teaser rate. After the initial low-interest period ends and the new interest rate kicks in, the monthly payments that the borrower must make may increase, possibly by a significant amount.

Adjustable-rate mortgages make economic sense for some borrowers, especially if interest rates are expected to go down in the future. ARMs can help people own a home sooner than they may have been able to otherwise, or make sense for borrowers who cannot afford a high loan payment in the present but expect a significant increase in income in the future that would allow them to afford higher monthly payments. Furthermore, the interest rate on ARMs tends to follow short-term interest rates in the economy; if the gap between short-term and long-term rates gets very wide, it might make sense for borrowers to choose an ARM even if they expect interest rates to rise in the future. Finally, in markets with rising property values, borrowers with ARMs may be able to refinance their mortgages to avoid higher interest rates or large increases in monthly payments. However, if home prices fall, refinancing the mortgage or selling the home to pay off the debt may not be feasible, leaving the homeowner with higher mortgage payments if interest rates rise.

Zero-Downpayment or Low-Downpayment Loans

As the name suggests, zero-downpayment and low-downpayment loans require either no downpayment or a significantly lower downpayment than has traditionally been required. These types of loans make it easier for homebuyers who do not have a lot of cash up-front to purchase a home. This type of loan may be especially useful in areas where home prices are rising more rapidly than income, because it allows borrowers without enough cash for a large downpayment to enter markets they could not otherwise afford. However, a low- or no-downpayment loan also means that families have little or no equity in their homes in the early phases of the mortgage, making it difficult to sell the home or refinance the mortgage in response to a change in circumstances if home prices decline. Such loans may also mean that a homeowner takes out a larger mortgage than he or she would otherwise.

---

[9] Even if the interest rate remains the same or decreases, it is possible for monthly payments to increase if prior payments were subject to an interest rate cap or a payment cap. This is because unpaid interest that would have accrued if not for the cap can be added to the principal loan amount, resulting in negative amortization. For more information on the many variations of adjustable rate mortgages, see The Federal Reserve Board, *Consumer Handbook on Adjustable Rate Mortgages*, http://www.federalreserve.gov/pubs/arms/arms_english htm#drop.

Interest-Only Loans and Negative Amortization Loans

With an interest-only loan, borrowers pay only the interest on a mortgage—but no part of the principal—for a set period of time. This option increases the homeowner's monthly payments in the future, after the interest-only period ends and the principal amortizes. These types of loans limit a household's ability to build equity in its home, making it difficult to sell or refinance the home in response to a change in circumstances if home prices are declining.

With a negative amortization loan, borrowers have the option to pay less than the full amount of the interest due for a set period of time. The loan "negatively amortizes" as the remaining interest is added to the outstanding loan balance. Like interest-only loans, this option increases future monthly mortgage payments when the principal and the balance of the interest amortizes. These types of loans can be useful in markets where property values are rising rapidly, because borrowers can enter the market and then use the equity gained from rising home prices to refinance into loans with better terms before payments increase. They can also make sense for borrowers who currently have low incomes but expect a significant increase in income in the future. However, when home prices stagnate or fall, interest-only loans and negative amortization loans can leave borrowers with negative equity, making it difficult to refinance or sell the home to pay the mortgage debt.

Alt-A Loans

Alt-A loans are mortgages that are similar to prime loans, but for one or more reasons do not qualify for prime interest rates. One example of an Alt-A loan is a low-documentation or no-documentation loan. These are loans to borrowers with good credit scores but little or no income or asset documentation. Although no-documentation loans allow for more fraudulent activity on the part of both borrowers and lenders, they may be useful for borrowers with income that is difficult to document, such as those who are self-employed or work on commission. Other examples of Alt-A loans are loans with high loan-to-value ratios or loans to borrowers with credit scores that are too low for a prime loan but high enough to avoid a subprime loan. In all of these cases, the borrower is charged a higher interest rate than he or she would be charged with a prime loan to compensate for the increased credit risk of the borrower.

While all of these types of loans often make sense for certain borrowers in certain circumstances, many of these loan features began to be used more widely and may have played a role in the recent increase in foreclosure rates. Some homeowners were current on their mortgages before their monthly payments increased due to interest rate resets or the end of option periods. Some built up little equity in their homes because they were not paying down the principal balance of their loan or because they had not made a downpayment. Stagnant or falling home prices in many regions also hampered borrowers' ability to build equity in their homes. Borrowers without sufficient equity find it difficult to take advantage of options such as refinancing into a more traditional mortgage if monthly payments become too high or selling the home if their personal circumstances change.

Types of Loan Workouts

When a household falls behind on its mortgage, there are options that lenders or mortgage servicers[10] may be able to employ as an alternative to beginning foreclosure proceedings. Some of these options, such as a short sale and a deed-in-lieu of foreclosure,[11] allow a homeowner to avoid the foreclosure process but still result in a household losing its home. This section describes methods of avoiding foreclosure that allow homeowners to keep their homes; these options generally take the form of repayment plans or loan modifications.

Repayment Plans

A repayment plan allows a delinquent borrower to become up-to-date on his or her loan by paying back the payments he or she has missed, along with any accrued late fees. This is different from a loan modification, which changes one or more of the terms of the loan (such as the interest rate). Under a repayment plan, the missed payments and late fees may be paid back after the rest of the loan is paid off, or they may be added to the existing monthly payments. The first option increases the time that it will take for a borrower to pay back the loan, but his or her monthly payments will remain the same. The second option may result in an increase in monthly payments. Repayment plans may be a good option for homeowners who experienced a temporary loss of income but are now financially stable. However, since they do not generally make payments more affordable, repayment plans are unlikely to help homeowners with unaffordable loans avoid foreclosure in the long term.

Interest Rate Reductions

One form of a loan modification is when the lender voluntarily lowers the interest rate on a mortgage. This is different from a refinance, in which a borrower takes out a new mortgage with a lower interest rate and uses the proceeds from the new loan to pay off the old loan. Unlike refinancing, a borrower does not have to pay closing costs or qualify for a new loan to get a mortgage modification with an interest rate reduction, which can make interest rate reductions a good option for borrowers who owe more on their mortgages than their homes are worth. With an interest rate reduction, the interest rate can be reduced permanently, or it can be reduced for a period of time before increasing again to a certain fixed point. Lenders can also freeze interest rates at their current level in order to avoid impending interest rate resets on adjustable rate mortgages. Interest rate modifications are relatively costly to the lender or mortgage investor because they reduce the amount of interest income that the lender or investor will receive, but they can be effective at reducing monthly payments to an affordable level.

---

[10] Mortgage lenders are the organizations that make mortgage loans to individuals. Often, the mortgage is managed by a company known as a servicer; servicers usually have the most contact with the borrower, and are responsible for actions such as collecting mortgage payments, initiating foreclosures, and communicating with troubled borrowers. The servicer can be an affiliate of the original mortgage lender or can be a separate company. Many mortgages are repackaged into mortgage-backed securities (MBS) that are sold to institutional investors. Servicers are usually subject to contracts with mortgage lenders and MBS investors that may limit their ability to undertake loan workouts or modifications; the scope of such contracts and the obligations that servicers must meet vary widely.

[11] In a short sale, a household sells its home for less than the amount it owes on its mortgage, and the lender generally accepts the proceeds from the sale as payment in full on the mortgage even though it is taking a loss. A deed-in-lieu of foreclosure refers to the practice of a borrower turning the deed to the house over to the lender, which accepts the deed as payment of the mortgage debt. However, in some cases, the borrower may still be liable for the remaining outstanding mortgage debt when a short sale or a deed-in-lieu is utilized.

Extended Loan Term/Extended Amortization

Another option for lowering monthly mortgage payments is extending the amount of time over which the loan is paid back. While extending the loan term increases the total cost of the mortgage for the borrower because more interest will accrue, it allows monthly payments to be smaller because they are paid over a longer period of time. Most mortgages in the U.S. have an initial loan term of 25 or 30 years; extending the loan term from 30 to 40 years, for example, could result in a lower monthly mortgage payment for the borrower.

Principal Forbearance

Principal forbearance means that a lender or servicer removes part of the principal from the portion of the loan balance that is subject to interest, thereby lowering borrowers' monthly payments by reducing the amount of interest owed. The portion of the principal that is subject to forbearance still needs to be repaid by the borrower in full, usually after the interest-bearing part of the loan is paid off or when the home is sold. Because principal forbearance does not actually change any of the loan terms, it resembles a repayment plan more than a loan modification.

Principal Write-Downs/Principal Forgiveness

A principal write-down or principal forgiveness is a type of mortgage modification that lowers borrowers' monthly payments by forgiving a portion of the loan's principal balance. The forgiven portion of the principal never needs to be repaid. Because the borrower now owes less, his or her monthly payment will be smaller. This option may be costlier for lenders or mortgage investors than other types of mortgage modifications, but it can help borrowers achieve affordable monthly payments, as well as increase the equity that borrowers have in their homes and therefore increase their desire to stay current on the mortgage and avoid foreclosure.[12]

Current Foreclosure Prevention Initiatives

In the past several years, the federal government has implemented a variety of initiatives to attempt to address the high rates of residential mortgage foreclosures. Some of these initiatives have been enacted by Congress, while others have been created administratively by both the Bush and Obama administrations. This section describes federal foreclosure prevention initiatives that are currently active. **Appendix B** describes additional foreclosure prevention initiatives that have been implemented in recent years, but that are no longer in effect.

In addition to federal efforts to address mortgage foreclosures, many state and local governments have also implemented a range of initiatives to reduce the number of foreclosures in recent years. The private sector has also pursued foreclosure prevention efforts, including creating the HOPE NOW Alliance, a voluntary alliance of mortgage servicers, lenders, investors, counseling

---

[12] Historically, one impediment to principal forgiveness has been that borrowers were required to claim the forgiven amount as income, and therefore had to pay taxes on that income. In December 2007, Congress passed legislation that temporarily excluded mortgage debt forgiven prior to January 1, 2010, from taxable income; the exclusion has since been extended to mortgage debt forgiven prior to January 1, 2014. For more information about the tax treatment of principal forgiveness, see CRS Report RL34212, *Analysis of the Tax Exclusion for Canceled Mortgage Debt Income*, by Mark P. Keightley and Erika K. Lunder.

agencies, and others that formed in October 2007 with the encouragement of the federal government to engage in active outreach efforts to troubled borrowers.[13] While many private lenders and mortgage servicers participate in federal foreclosure prevention initiatives, many also have their own programs or procedures in place to work with borrowers who are having difficulty making their mortgage payments. This report focuses on federal efforts to prevent foreclosure, and does not address these state, local, and private sector efforts.

Making Home Affordable

On February 18, 2009, President Obama announced the Making Home Affordable (MHA) program, aimed at helping homeowners who are having difficulty making their mortgage payments avoid foreclosure.[14] Making Home Affordable includes separate initiatives to make it easier for certain homeowners to refinance or modify their mortgages. These initiatives are known as the Home Affordable Refinance Program (HARP) and the Home Affordable Modification Program (HAMP), respectively, and each is described in the following subsections.

Home Affordable Refinance Program (HARP)

The refinancing initiative under MHA is the Home Affordable Refinance Program. HARP allows homeowners with mortgages owned or guaranteed by Fannie Mae or Freddie Mac[15] to refinance into loans with more favorable terms even if they owe more than 80% of the value of their homes. Generally, borrowers who owe more than 80% of the value of their homes have difficulty refinancing because they do not have enough equity in their homes. Because they cannot refinance their mortgages, they cannot take advantage of lower interest rates. By allowing borrowers who owe more than 80% of the value of their homes to refinance their mortgages, the plan is meant to help qualified borrowers lower their monthly mortgage payments to a level that is more affordable.[16] Originally, qualified borrowers were eligible to refinance under this program if they owed up to 105% of the value of their homes. In July 2009, the Administration announced that it would expand the program to include borrowers who owe up to 125% of the value of their homes. In October 2011, the Federal Housing Finance Agency (FHFA), Fannie's and Freddie's conservator, announced that it would remove the loan-to-value ratio cap entirely.

---

[13] For a full list of current members of the HOPE NOW Alliance, see the HOPE NOW website at https://www.hopenow.com/members.php.

[14] The program details originally referred to the program as the Homeowner Affordability and Stability Plan, or HASP. Further program details released on March 4, 2009, began referring to the plan as Making Home Affordable. More information on Making Home Affordable can be found http://www.treasury.gov/initiatives/financial-stability/TARP-Programs/housing/Pages/default.aspx.

[15] Fannie Mae and Freddie Mac are government-sponsored enterprises (GSEs) that were chartered by Congress to provide liquidity to the mortgage market. Rather than make loans directly, the GSEs buy loans made in the private market and either hold them in their own portfolios or securitize and sell them to investors. The GSEs were put under the conservatorship of FHFA on September 7, 2008. For more information on the GSEs in general, see CRS Report RL33756, *Fannie Mae and Freddie Mac: A Legal and Policy Overview*, by N. Eric Weiss and Michael V. Seitzinger, and for more information on the conservatorship, see CRS Report RS22950, *Fannie Mae and Freddie Mac in Conservatorship*, by Mark Jickling.

[16] The program is completely voluntary, and lenders are not required to refinance mortgages through HARP even if the mortgages meet all of the eligibility criteria.

In addition to having a mortgage owned or guaranteed by Fannie Mae or Freddie Mac,[17] a borrower must have a mortgage on a single-family home, the original mortgage must have been closed on or before May 31, 2009,[18] and the borrower must be current on the mortgage payments in order to be eligible for this program, among other eligibility criteria. Rather than targeting homeowners who are behind on their mortgage payments, this piece of the MHA plan targets homeowners who have kept up with their payments but have lost equity in their homes due to falling home prices. HARP is scheduled to end on December 31, 2015.[19]

Changes to HARP Announced in October 2011 ("HARP 2.0")

In October 2011, the Federal Housing Finance Agency (FHFA) announced a number of changes to HARP designed to allow more people to qualify for the program.[20] As discussed earlier, one of these changes removed the cap on the loan-to-value ratio, which had previously limited eligibility for the program to those with loan-to-value ratios up to 125%. Another change is that Fannie Mae and Freddie Mac have eliminated or reduced certain fees that are paid by borrowers who refinance through HARP. Fannie and Freddie will also waive certain representations and warranties made by lenders on the original loans, which may make lenders more likely to participate in HARP by releasing them from some responsibility for any defects in the original loan. The changes also encourage greater use of automated valuation models instead of property appraisals in order to streamline the refinancing process. Finally, as part of these HARP changes, FHFA extended the end date for the program to December 31, 2013, although it has since been extended again, to December 31, 2015.

Fannie Mae and Freddie Mac have each released their own guidance governing how the HARP changes will be implemented for loans that they own or guarantee.[21] Many of these changes

---

[17] Borrowers can look up whether their loan is owned by Fannie Mae or Freddie Mac at http://makinghomeaffordable.gov/loan_lookup html.

[18] Originally, the original mortgage must have been delivered to Fannie Mae and Freddie Mac on or prior to May 31, 2009. Because there is often a lag between when a mortgage closes and when it is sold and delivered to Fannie Mae or Freddie Mac, this meant that some mortgages that had closed on or prior to May 31, 2009, may not have been eligible if they had not also been delivered to Fannie or Freddie prior to that date. In October 2013, Fannie Mae and Freddie Mac each announced that HARP would now be open to mortgages that closed on or prior to May 31, 2009, regardless of the date that the mortgage was delivered. See Fannie Mae Selling Guide Announcement SEL-2013-08, dated October 22, 2013, at https://www.fanniemae.com/content/announcement/sel1308.pdf; and Freddie Mac, "Revised Eligibility Date for Relief Refinance Mortgages," October 22, 2013, at http://www.freddiemac.com/singlefamily/news/2013/1022_revised_eligibility_date.html.

[19] HARP was originally scheduled to expire on June 10, 2010. The Federal Housing Finance Agency has extended the program four times. In March 2010, FHFA announced that it was extending the program until June 30, 2011. In March 2011, FHFA announced that it was extending the program by another year, until June 30, 2012. In October 2011, FHFA announced that it would extend the program until December 31, 2013, and in April 2013, it announced that it would extend the program until December 31, 2015. See the following Federal Housing Finance Agency press releases: "FHFA Extends Refinance Program by One Year," March 1, 2010, http://fhfa.gov/webfiles/15466/HARPEXTENDED3110%5b1%5d.pdf; "FHFA Extends Refinance Program by One Year," March 11, 2011, http://fhfa.gov/webfiles/20399/HarpExtended0311R.pdf; "FHFA, Fannie Mae and Freddie Mac Announce HARP Changes to Reach More Borrowers," October 24, 2011, http://fhfa.gov/webfiles/22721/HARP_release_102411_Final.pdf, and "FHFA Extends HARP to 2015," April 11, 2013, http://www.fhfa.gov/webfiles/25112/HARPextensionPRFINAL41113.pdf.

[20] Federal Housing Finance Agency, "FHFA, Fannie Mae and Freddie Mac Announce HARP Changes to Reach More Borrowers," press release, October 24, 2011, http://fhfa.gov/webfiles/22721/HARP_release_102411_Final.pdf.

[21] Fannie Mae's detailed guidance on the program changes can be found at https://www.efanniemae.com/sf/guides/ssg/annltrs/pdf/2011/sel1112.pdf. Freddie Mac's detailed guidance on the changes can be found at (continued...)

became effective in December 2011 or January 2012; however, specific changes went into effect on different dates, and the effective dates can vary between Fannie Mae and Freddie Mac. Individual lenders might also vary in when they implemented the program changes, or, since HARP is not mandatory, whether they adopted all of the changes allowed by FHFA.

In addition to these changes to HARP, legislation has been introduced in both the 112th and 113th Congresses to make further changes to the program in an attempt to expand access to HARP to more borrowers. Furthermore, some policymakers have proposed a HARP-like program to make it easier for borrowers in negative equity positions whose loans are not backed by Fannie Mae or Freddie Mac to refinance. For a more in-depth discussion of such proposals, see CRS Report R42480, *Reduce, Refinance, and Rent? The Economic Incentives, Risks, and Ramifications of Housing Market Policy Options*, by Sean M. Hoskins.

HARP Results to Date

The Administration originally estimated that HARP could help up to between 4 million and 5 million homeowners. According to the Federal Housing Finance Agency (FHFA), Fannie Mae and Freddie Mac refinanced nearly 2.9 million loans with loan-to-value ratios above 80% through August 2013.[22] The majority of these mortgages (over 2 million) had loan-to-value ratios between 80% and 105%, while just fewer than 500,000 mortgages had loan-to-value ratios above 105% up to 125% and nearly 400,000 mortgages had loan-to-value ratios above 125%. **Table 1** shows the number of HARP refinances completed by Fannie Mae and Freddie Mac since the program began.

Table 1. Number of HARP Refinances

As of August 2013

	Fannie Mae	Freddie Mac	Total
LTV over 80% up to 105%	1,202,164	818,131	2,020,295
LTV over 105% up to 125%	273,655	219,999	493,654
LTV over 125%	221,890	151,017	372,907
Total	1,697,709	1,189,147	2,886,856

Source: Federal Housing Finance Agency Refinance Report, August 2013.

Home Affordable Modification Program (HAMP)

The mortgage modification piece of the Administration's Making Home Affordable program is the Home Affordable Modification Program (HAMP).[23] Through HAMP, the government provides financial incentives to participating mortgage servicers that provide loan modifications

---

(...continued)

http://www.freddiemac.com/sell/guide/bulletins/pdf/bll1122.pdf.

[22] Federal Housing Finance Agency, *Refinance Report: August 2013*, p. 3, http://www.fhfa.gov/webfiles/25620/August2013RefiReport.pdf.

[23] HAMP shares many features of earlier foreclosure prevention programs, such as the Federal Deposit Insurance Corporation's plan to modify loans held by the failed IndyMac Bank, and Fannie Mae's and Freddie Mac's Streamlined Modification Program. These programs are described in detail in **Appendix B**.

---

to eligible troubled borrowers in order to reduce the borrowers' monthly mortgage payments to no more than 31% of their monthly income.[24] Modifications can be made through HAMP until December 31, 2015,[25] unless the program is terminated before that date.[26]

In order to qualify for HAMP, a borrower must have a mortgage on a single-family (one-to-four unit) property that was originated on or before January 1, 2009, must live in the home as his or her primary residence, and must have an unpaid principal balance on the mortgage that is no greater than $729,750 for a one-unit property. Furthermore, the borrower must currently be paying more than 31% of his or her monthly gross income toward mortgage payments, and must be experiencing a financial hardship that makes it difficult to remain current on the mortgage. Borrowers need not already be delinquent on their mortgages in order to qualify, but default must be "reasonably foreseeable."

Servicers participating in HAMP conduct a "net present value test" (NPV test) on eligible mortgages that compares the expected financial returns to investors from doing a loan modification to the expected financial returns from pursuing a foreclosure. If the expected returns from a loan modification are greater than those from foreclosure, servicers are required to reduce borrowers' payments to no more than 38% of monthly income. The government then shares half the cost of reducing borrowers' payments from 38% of monthly income to 31% of monthly income. Servicers reduce borrowers' payments by reducing the interest rate, extending the loan term, and forbearing principal, in that order, as necessary to reach the payment ratio. (Servicers are permitted to reduce mortgage principal as part of a HAMP modification, but are not required to do so.) Servicers can reduce interest rates to as low as 2%. The new interest rate must remain in place for five years; after five years, if the interest rate is below the market rate at the time the modification agreement was completed, the interest rate can rise by one percentage point per year until it reaches that market rate. Borrowers must make modified payments on time during a three-month trial period before the modification can be converted to permanent status.

The Home Affordable Modification Program is voluntary,[27] but once a servicer signs an agreement to participate in the program, that servicer is bound by the rules of the program and is required to modify eligible mortgages according to the program guidelines. The government provides incentives to servicers, investors, and borrowers for participation. Servicers receive an

---

[24] Treasury's requirements governing HAMP for mortgages that are not backed by Fannie Mae or Freddie Mac are available in a handbook that is updated periodically to incorporate new guidance or changes to the program. That handbook is available at https://www.hmpadmin.com/portal/index.jsp. HAMP guidance related to mortgages owned or guaranteed by Fannie Mae or Freddie Mac can be found on those entities' respective websites. In general, the HAMP guidance for GSE mortgages is similar to the guidance for non-GSE mortgages, but there are some differences.

[25] The program was originally scheduled to end on December 31, 2012. However, in January 2012 the Administration announced that it would extend the deadline to December 31, 2013, and in May 2013 the Administration announced that it would extend the program until December 31, 2015. See http://www.treasury.gov/connect/blog/Pages/Expanding-our-efforts-to-help-more-homeowners-and-strengthen-hard-hit-communities.aspx and http://portal hud.gov/hudportal/HUD?src=/press/press_releases_media_advisories/2013/HUDNo.13-083.

[26] During the 112th Congress, the House passed H.R. 839, which, if enacted, would have terminated the program and rescinded unobligated funds. Borrowers who were currently participating in the program would not have been affected if this bill had become law. CBO estimated that H.R. 839 would have reduced direct federal spending by $1.4 billion over a 10-year period. (See Congressional Budget Office, *H.R. 839 HAMP Termination Act of 2011*, cost estimate, March 11, 2011, http://cbo.gov/ftpdocs/120xx/doc12097/hr839.pdf.) The bill was not considered by the Senate.

[27] Servicers of mortgages backed by Fannie Mae or Freddie Mac are required to participate in HAMP for those mortgages. Companies that received funding through Troubled Assets Relief Program (TARP) or Financial Stability Plan (FSP) programs announced after the announcement of Making Home Affordable are also required to participate in HAMP.

---

upfront incentive payment for each successful permanent loan modification, an additional payment for modifications made for borrowers who are not yet delinquent, and a "pay-for-success" payment for up to three years if the borrower remains current after the modification. The borrower can also receive a "pay-for-success" incentive payment (in the form of principal reduction) for up to five years if he or she remains current after the modification is finalized. Investors receive the payment cost-share incentive (that is, the government's payment of half the cost of reducing the monthly mortgage payment from 38% to 31% of monthly income), and can receive incentive payments for loans modified before a borrower becomes delinquent.

HAMP has been modified or updated a number of times since it was first established, including changes to the program's rules and the implementation of additional HAMP programs to attempt to assist certain groups, such as unemployed borrowers or borrowers with negative equity. These changes are described in the "Additional HAMP Components and Major Program Changes" section.

HAMP Funding

The Administration originally estimated that HAMP would cost $75 billion. Of this amount, $50 billion was to come from Troubled Asset Relief Program (TARP) funds,[28] and $25 billion was to come from Fannie Mae and Freddie Mac for the costs of modifying mortgages that those entities own or guarantee.[29]

Treasury has since revised its estimate of the amount of TARP funds that will be used for HAMP, and has used some of the $50 billion originally allocated to HAMP to help pay for other foreclosure-related programs (the Hardest Hit Fund and the FHA Refinance program, both described in later sections of this report).Treasury has now committed $38.5 billion of TARP funds to its foreclosure prevention programs, rather than the initial $50 billion. Of this amount, nearly $30 billion is committed to HAMP and its related programs, $7.6 billion is committed to the Hardest Hit Fund, and up to just over $1 billion is committed to the FHA Short Refinance Program.[30]

As of November 14, 2013, nearly $10 billion of the funding committed to these programs has been disbursed. Of that amount, $6.8 billion has been disbursed for HAMP and its related programs.[31]

---

[28] TARP was authorized by the Emergency Economic Stabilization Act of 2008 (P.L. 110-343). For more information on TARP, see CRS Report R41427, *Troubled Asset Relief Program (TARP): Implementation and Status*, by Baird Webel.

[29] Department of the Treasury, Section 105(a) Troubled Assets Relief Program Report to Congress for the Period February 1, 2009 to February 28, 2009, p. 1, available at http://www.financialstability.gov/docs/105CongressionalReports/105aReport_03062009.pdf.

[30] Originally, Treasury committed just over $8 billion to the FHA Short Refinance Program. In response to lower-than-anticipated program participation, and therefore fewer defaults, Treasury has reduced the maximum amount it will spend on this program to just over $1 billion. See Treasury's *Troubled Asset Relief Program Monthly Report to Congress – March 2013*, p. 21, http://www.treasury.gov/initiatives/financial-stability/reports/Documents/March%202013%20Monthly%20Report%20to%20Congress.pdf.

[31] U.S. Department of the Treasury, *Daily TARP Update for 11/14/2013*, http://www.treasury.gov/initiatives/financial-stability/reports/Documents/Daily%20TARP%20Update%20-%2011.14.2013.pdf.

HAMP Results to Date

The Administration originally estimated that HAMP could eventually help up to between 3 million and 4 million homeowners. The Treasury Department releases monthly reports detailing the program's progress. These reports offer a variety of information, including the number of overall trial and permanent modifications made under HAMP and the number of each that are currently active, the number of trial and permanent modifications made by individual servicers, and the number of trial and permanent modifications underway in each state.[32] (As noted earlier, borrowers must successfully complete a three-month trial period before the modification is converted to permanent status.)

According to the September 2013 monthly report, there were about 969,000 active HAMP modifications as of the end of September 2013. Of these, about 60,000 were active trial modifications and about 909,000 were active permanent modifications.[33] **Table 2** shows the number of HAMP trial modifications that have started since the program began, along with the number of each that are currently active.

Table 2. Number of HAMP Modifications
As of September 2013

	Trial Modifications	Permanent Modifications	Total
All Started	2,109,130	1,268,635	N/A
Currently Active	59,795	909,220	969,015

Source: Making Home Affordable Program Performance Report Through September 2013.

Figure 2 illustrates the total number of modifications, both trial and permanent, that have been active in each month since January 2010. Since mid-2010, the total number of active modifications has gradually increased, driven by an increasing number of active permanent modifications. The total number of active trial modifications has generally been decreasing as trial modifications convert to permanent status or are canceled, and fewer new trial modifications have been started as the program has aged.

---

[32] Treasury's monthly reports on HAMP can be found at http://www.treasury.gov/initiatives/financial-stability/reports/Pages/Making-Home-Affordable-Program-Performance-Report.aspx.

[33] U.S. Department of the Treasury, *Making Home Affordable Program Servicer Performance Report Through September 2013*, p. 3, http://www.treasury.gov/initiatives/financial-stability/reports/Documents/September%202013%20MHA%20Report%20Final.pdf.

Figure 2. Total Active HAMP Modifications by Month

January 2010–September 2013

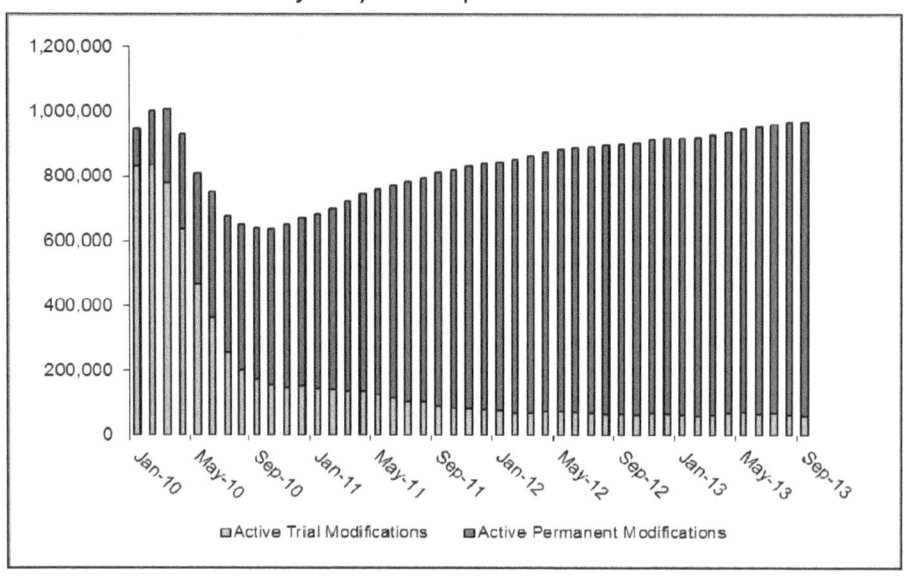

Source: Figure created by CRS based on data from Treasury's monthly Making Home Affordable Program Servicer Performance Reports.

Figure 3 shows the number of new HAMP trial modifications and new HAMP permanent modifications that have started in each month from January 2010 to the present. As the figure illustrates, the number of new trials declined sharply during the beginning of 2010. This was probably at least in part due to a program change that required servicers to verify a borrower's income information before approving a trial modification, rather than allowing servicers to verify borrower income during the trial period but before the modification became permanent. (This change is described further in the following section.)

From around May 2010 through the end of 2011, the number of new trial modifications that began each month fluctuated within a range of between about 20,000 and 40,000. Since then, the number of new trial modifications that have started each month has generally been fewer than 20,000. The number of new permanent modifications started each month has decreased from a peak of 68,000 in April 2010. Like the number of new trial modifications, the number of new permanent modifications started each month in 2011 was generally between 20,000 and 40,000, and since then has generally been between 10,000 and 20,000.

Figure 3. New Trial and Permanent HAMP Modifications by Month

January 2010–September 2013

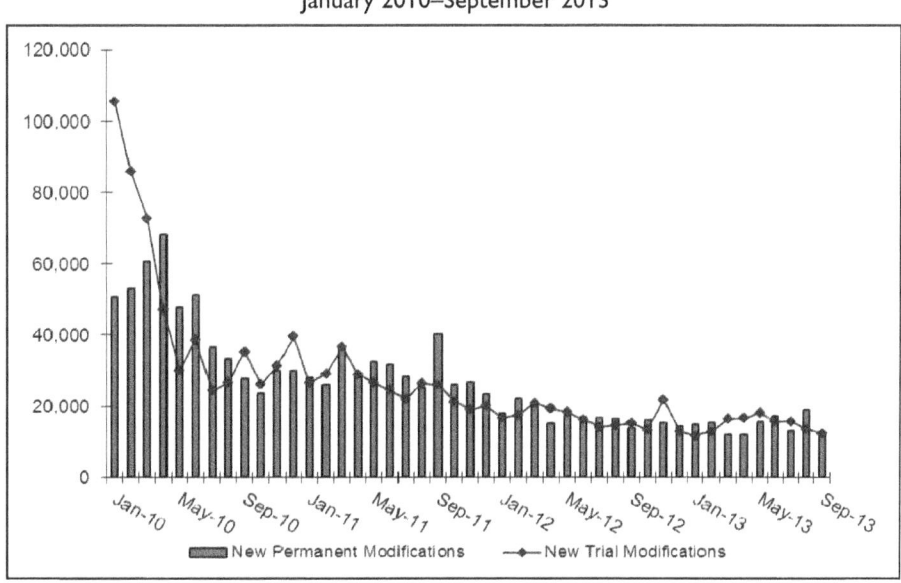

Source: Figure created by CRS based on data from Treasury's monthly Making Home Affordable Program Servicer Performance Reports.

Conversion of Trial Modifications to Permanent Status

After HAMP had been in place for several months, many observers began to express concern at the high number of trial modifications that were being canceled rather than converting to permanent status and the length of time that it was taking for trial modifications to become permanent. In order for a modification to become permanent, a borrower must make all of the trial period payments on time, and must submit all necessary documentation (such as tax returns, proof of income, and a signed Modification Agreement) to the servicer. In response to these concerns, Treasury took a number of steps to attempt to facilitate the conversion of trial modifications to permanent modifications.

One major change implemented by Treasury was requiring servicers to have documented income information from borrowers before offering a trial modification. This change has been in place since June 2010.[34] When the program first began, servicers had been allowed to begin a trial modification based on stated income information in order to get trial modifications started more quickly, but the servicers had to verify this information in order for a modification to become permanent. Requiring verified information before a trial modification could begin was expected to result in more trial modifications converting to permanent modifications going forward. As of September 2013, Treasury reported that 88% of trial modifications that had begun since June 1, 2010 had converted to permanent status.[35]

---

[34] For Treasury's guidance on this change, see Supplemental Directive 10-01, "Home Affordable Modification Program – Program Update and Resolution of Active Trial Modifications," January 28, 2010, https://www.hmpadmin.com/portal/programs/docs/hamp_servicer/sd1001.pdf.

[35] U.S. Department of the Treasury, *Making Home Affordable Program Performance Report Through September 2013*, p. 16, http://www.treasury.gov/initiatives/financial-stability/reports/Documents/
(continued...)

Other steps that Treasury took included outreach efforts to borrowers to help them understand and meet the program's documentation requirements and increased reporting requirements and monitoring of servicers.[36] Beginning with the April 2010 monthly report, Treasury began reporting conversion rates of trial modifications to permanent modifications for individual servicers, along with other metrics related to individual servicers' performance.

Treasury's Assessments of Servicer Performance

In the April 2011 monthly report, Treasury released comprehensive results of an examination of the performance of the ten largest servicers participating in HAMP, and indicated that it would continue to release the results of these servicer assessments on a quarterly basis. As a result of this examination, Treasury announced that it was going to withhold incentive payments to three of the largest participating servicers due to findings that the servicers' performance under the program was not meeting Treasury's standards. The servicers, Bank of America, JP Morgan Chase, and Wells Fargo, were all found to need "substantial" improvement in several areas.[37] Treasury said that it would reinstate the incentive payments when the servicers' performance improved and was no longer found to need substantial improvement. The remaining six of the ten largest servicers were found to need moderate improvement, but Treasury did not withhold incentive payments from those servicers.[38]

The results of the next quarterly servicer assessments, included in the July 2011 monthly report, found that Bank of America and JP Morgan Chase continued to need substantial improvement,[39] and the October 2011 monthly report found that only one servicer, JP Morgan Chase, was found to need substantial improvement.[40] By the January 2012 monthly report, no servicers were found to need substantial improvement; seven were found to need moderate improvement, and two were found to need minor improvement.[41] As of the July 2013 monthly report, seven servicers were included in the assessment, and all were found to need moderate improvement.[42]

(...continued)

September%202013%20MHA%20Report%20Final.pdf.

[36] U.S. Department of the Treasury and U.S. Department of Housing and Urban Development, "Obama Administration Kicks Off Mortgage Modification Conversion Drive," press release, November 30, 2009, available at http://treas.gov/press/releases/tg421 htm.

[37] A fourth servicer, Ocwen, was found to need substantial improvement as well, but Treasury did not withhold incentive payments from Ocwen at that time due to a finding that its performance was partially due to a loan portfolio that it had bought from another company.

[38] U.S. Department of the Treasury, *Making Home Affordable Program Performance Report through April 2011*, June 9, 2011. Servicer assessment results begin on page 14. All monthly reports can be found at http://www.treasury.gov/initiatives/financial-stability/results/MHA-Reports/Pages/default.aspx.

[39] U.S. Department of the Treasury, *Making Home Affordable Program Performance Report through July 2011*, September 1, 2011. Servicer assessment results begin on page 16.

[40] U.S. Department of the Treasury, *Making Home Affordable Program Performance Report through October 2011*, December 7, 2011. Servicer assessment results begin on page 16.

[41] U.S. Department of the Treasury, *Making Home Affordable Program Performance Report through January 2012*, Servicer assessment results begin on page 18.

[42] U.S. Department of the Treasury, *Making Home Affordable Program Performance Report through July 2013*, p. 21.

Additional HAMP Components and Major Program Changes

Since the program's announcement, Treasury has announced several changes to HAMP, as well as a number of additional components or subprograms that operate under HAMP. The subprograms that operate under HAMP include the following:

Second Lien Modification Program (2MP)[43]

Many borrowers have second mortgages on their homes. Second mortgages can cause problems for loan modification programs because (1) modifying the first lien may not reduce households' total monthly mortgage payments to an affordable level if the second mortgage remains unmodified, and (2) holders of primary mortgages are often hesitant to modify the mortgage if the second mortgage holder does not agree to re-subordinate the second mortgage to the first mortgage, or to modify the second mortgage as well. Under 2MP, if the servicer of the second lien is participating in 2MP, then that servicer must agree either to modify the second lien in accordance with program guidelines, or to extinguish the second lien entirely in exchange for a lump sum payment, when a borrower's first mortgage is modified under HAMP. (Servicers sign up to participate in 2MP separately from signing up to participate in HAMP.)

Under 2MP, if a servicer modifies a second lien, it can receive an upfront incentive payment of $500. Servicers can also receive "pay-for-success" payments of up to $250 per year for up to three years, if the monthly second mortgage payments are reduced by 6% or more and if the borrower remains current on both the HAMP modification and the 2MP modification. Borrowers can receive annual "pay-for-success" payments of up to $250 per year for up to five years (in the form of principal reduction) if the second mortgage payments have been reduced by 6% or more and if the borrowers remain current on both the HAMP and 2MP modifications. Investors can receive compensation for modified second liens according to a cost-sharing formula. Servicers can also receive incentives for extinguishing, rather than modifying, second liens, and investors receive compensation for extinguished second liens according to a cost-sharing formula.

Treasury reports that about 77,000 second-lien modifications are active under 2MP as of September 2013.[44]

Home Affordable Foreclosure Alternatives Program (HAFA)[45]

Through the Home Affordable Foreclosure Alternatives Program (HAFA), when a borrower meets the basic eligibility criteria for HAMP, but does not ultimately qualify for a modification, does not successfully complete the trial period, or defaults on a HAMP modification, participating servicers can receive incentive payments for completing a short sale or a deed-in-lieu of foreclosure as an alternative to foreclosure.[46] Servicers can receive incentive payments of $1,500

---

[43] Servicer guidelines on 2MP are available at https://www.hmpadmin.com/portal/programs/second_lien.html.

[44] U.S. Department of the Treasury, *Making Home Affordable Program Servicer Performance Report Through September 2013*, p. 4, http://www.treasury.gov/initiatives/financial-stability/reports/Documents/September%202013%20MHA%20Report%20Final.pdf.

[45] Servicer guidelines on HAFA are available at https://www.hmpadmin.com/portal/programs/foreclosure_alternatives.html.

[46] Short sales and deeds-in-lieu are described in footnote 11. Under HAFA, the lender must agree to accept the proceeds of the short sale or the deed and property as full payment of the mortgage debt, and may not pursue borrowers (continued...)

---

for each short sale or deed-in-lieu that is successfully executed, and borrowers can receive incentive payments of $3,000 to help with relocation expenses.[47] Investors can receive partial reimbursement, up to a maximum of $5,000, if they agree to share a portion of the proceeds of the short sale with any subordinate lienholders.[48] (The subordinate lienholders, in turn, must release their liens on the property and waive all claims against the borrower for the unpaid balance of the subordinate mortgages.) In order to attempt to streamline the process of short sales and deeds-in-lieu of foreclosure under HAFA, Treasury provides standardized documentation and processes for participating servicers to use. HAFA became active on April 5, 2010, although servicers had the option to begin implementing the program before this date.

Treasury reports that about 226,000 HAFA transactions have been completed as of September 2013.[49] Most of these transactions have been short sales rather than deeds-in-lieu of foreclosure.

Home Affordable Unemployment Program (UP)

On March 26, 2010, the Administration announced the Home Affordable Unemployment Program (UP), which targets borrowers who are unemployed. Under UP, participating servicers are required to offer forbearance periods to unemployed borrowers who apply for HAMP and meet the UP eligibility criteria before evaluating those borrowers for HAMP. The forbearance period lasts for a minimum of twelve months, or until the borrower becomes re-employed.[50] Borrowers' mortgage payments are lowered to 31% or less of their monthly income through principal forbearance during this time period. After the forbearance period ends, it is expected that some borrowers will have regained employment and will not need further assistance. Other borrowers, such as those who are re-employed but at a lower salary, may be able to qualify for a regular HAMP modification. Still other borrowers may qualify for a foreclosure alternative such as a short sale or a deed-in-lieu of foreclosure, and some borrowers ultimately may not be able to avoid foreclosure. Participating servicers were required to begin offering forbearance plans to qualified unemployed borrowers by July 1, 2010, but could choose to implement the program earlier.[51]

(...continued)

for any remaining amounts owed on the mortgage. Short sales and deeds-in-lieu have a negative impact on a borrower's credit, but they may result in fewer negative consequences overall for the borrower than a foreclosure.

[47] Treasury has increased the amount of incentive compensation offered under HAFA to these amounts since the program was first announced.

[48] Supplemental Directive 12-07, "Home Affordable Foreclosure Alternatives Program – Policy Update," November 1, 2012, p. 8, https://www.hmpadmin.com/portal/programs/docs/hafa/sd1207.pdf.

[49] U.S. Department of the Treasury, *Making Home Affordable Program Servicer Performance Report Through September 2013*, p. 5, http://www.treasury.gov/initiatives/financial-stability/reports/Documents/September%202013%20MHA%20Report%20Final.pdf.

[50] Originally, the forbearance period was three months. Treasury extended it to twelve months in Supplemental Directive 11-07, *Making Home Affordable Program – Expansion of Unemployment Forbearance*, July 25, 2011, available at https://www.hmpadmin.com/portal/programs/docs/hamp_servicer/sd1107.pdf. The change became effective on October 1, 2011.

[51] The original detailed guidelines on the Home Affordable Unemployment Program were released in Supplemental Directive 10-04 on May 11, 2010. These guidelines are available at https://www.hmpadmin.com/portal/docs/hamp_servicer/sd1004.pdf. Updated guidance can be found in Treasury's Making Home Affordable Handbook, available at https://www.hmpadmin.com/portal/index.jsp.

Treasury reports that nearly 36,000 UP forbearance plans have been started as of September 2013.[52]

Principal Reduction Alternative (PRA)

Another change to HAMP announced on March 26, 2010, is the Principal Reduction Alternative (PRA), in which participating servicers are required to consider reducing principal balances as part of HAMP modifications for homeowners who owe at least 115% of the value of their home. Servicers will have to run two net present value tests for these borrowers: the first will be the standard NPV test, and the second will include principal reduction. If the net present value of the modification is higher under the test that includes principal reduction, servicers have the option to reduce principal. However, they are not required to do so. If the principal is reduced, the amount of the principal reduction will initially be treated as principal forbearance; the forborne amount will then be forgiven in three equal amounts over three years as long as the borrower remains current on his or her mortgage payments. The Administration will also offer incentives to servicers specifically for reducing principal. The PRA went into effect on October 1, 2010.[53] According to Treasury, about 119,000 PRA modifications were active as of September 2013. Nearly 15,000 of these are active trial modifications, and nearly 105,000 are active permanent modifications.[54]

Home Price Decline Protection Incentives

While not its own subprogram under HAMP, the HAMP guidelines also offer additional financial incentives to encourage modifications in markets where home prices are continuing to fall. These incentives are available to investors in connection with successful modifications in areas with declining home prices, provided that the borrower's monthly mortgage payment is reduced by at least 6%. The calculation of these incentive payments takes into account the recent rate of home price declines in the area where the home is located and the unpaid principal balance of the mortgage.

HAMP "Tier 2"

In early 2012, Treasury announced a number of expansions to HAMP, which it refers to as HAMP Tier 2.[55] HAMP Tier 2 expands eligibility for HAMP to certain borrowers who are not eligible for a standard HAMP modification (now referred to as HAMP Tier 1). Under HAMP Tier 2, borrowers still have to meet many of the basic HAMP eligibility criteria, including having a mortgage on a single-family property that was originated on or before January 1, 2009,

---

[52] U.S. Department of the Treasury, *Making Home Affordable Program Servicer Performance Report Through September 2013*, p. 4, http://www.treasury.gov/initiatives/financial-stability/reports/Documents/September%202013%20MHA%20Report%20Final.pdf.

[53] Detailed guidelines on the Principal Reduction Alternative were released in Supplemental Directive 10-05 on June 3, 2010. These guidelines are available at https://www.hmpadmin.com/portal/docs/hamp_servicer/sd1005.pdf.

[54] U.S. Department of the Treasury, *Making Home Affordable Program Servicer Performance Report Through September 2013*, p. 4, http://www.treasury.gov/initiatives/financial-stability/reports/Documents/September%202013%20MHA%20Report%20Final.pdf.

[55] Supplemental Directive 12-02, *Making Home Affordable Program – MHA Extension and Expansion*, March 9, 2012, https://www.hmpadmin.com/portal/programs/docs/hamp_servicer/sd1202.pdf.

experiencing a documented hardship, and having an unpaid principal balance below specified thresholds. However, borrowers might be able to qualify even if they do not meet other requirements to qualify for a standard HAMP modification, such as if they have a minimum debt-to-income ratio that is already below 31% or if they do not live in the home as a primary residence. For example, although HAMP Tier 1 requires borrowers to be owner-occupants, under HAMP Tier 2 certain types of rental properties are eligible for HAMP modifications. In order for a mortgage secured by a rental property to be eligible for HAMP Tier 2, the borrower must be delinquent on the mortgage (mortgages in "imminent default" are not eligible), the property must be currently occupied by a tenant or be vacant, and the borrower must certify that he or she intends to rent the property for at least five years (although at any point in that five year period the borrower can sell the home or choose to occupy it as a principal residence).

According to Treasury, a total of about 38,000 HAMP Tier 2 trial modifications had been started, and about 21,500 HAMP Tier 2 permanent modifications had been started, as of September 2013.[56]

Additional Changes

Treasury has also made a number of changes to the rules governing HAMP since the program began. Some of these changes have been minor, while others have made major changes to the program. Some notable changes include the following:

- When HAMP began, Treasury allowed servicers to approve borrowers for trial modifications on the basis of stated income information. Borrowers then had to submit documentation verifying their income information before the trial modification could convert to permanent status. In cases where the stated income information differed from the documented information, servicers often had to re-evaluate borrowers for the program (for example, by running a new NPV test), which sometimes resulted in borrowers who had been approved for a trial modification being denied for a permanent modification. Since June 1, 2010, Treasury requires all income information to be verified before a borrower can be approved for a trial period plan.[57] As described in the "HAMP Results to Date" section, this change was expected to result in a greater proportion of trial modifications converting to permanent status.

- The original HAMP guidelines prohibited servicers from conducting a foreclosure sale while they were evaluating a borrower for HAMP, or while a borrower was in a HAMP trial period. Servicers also were not allowed to refer new loans to foreclosure during the 30-day window that borrowers had to submit documentation indicating that they intended to accept a trial modification offer. However, foreclosures in process were allowed to continue, as long as no foreclosure sale occurred, and loans could be referred to foreclosure at the same time that a borrower was being evaluated for HAMP. Since June 1, 2010, Treasury prohibits servicers from referring eligible borrowers to foreclosure until

---

[56] U.S. Department of the Treasury, *Making Home Affordable Program Servicer Performance Report Through September 2013*, p. 3, http://www.treasury.gov/initiatives/financial-stability/reports/Documents/September%202013%20MHA%20Report%20Final.pdf.

[57] This change is described in detail in Treasury's Supplemental Directive 10-01, issued on January 28, 2010, and available at https://www.hmpadmin.com/portal/programs/docs/hamp_servicer/sd1001.pdf.

they have been evaluated for HAMP, or until reasonable outreach efforts have not been successful. Foreclosures that were already in process prior to this change were allowed to continue, although servicers had to take any actions that they had the authority to undertake to halt foreclosure proceedings for borrowers in trial modifications. Treasury also required enhanced disclosures to borrowers explaining that the home would not be sold in a foreclosure sale while the borrower was being evaluated for HAMP or was in a trial period.[58]

- Treasury has strengthened a number of other disclosure requirements since HAMP began, including requiring increased disclosures to borrowers who were denied a HAMP modification describing the reason for their denial. Treasury also provided more guidance on the outreach efforts that servicers must make to borrowers who may be eligible for HAMP.

- The Dodd-Frank Wall Street Reform and Consumer Protection Act (P.L. 111-203) made some changes to HAMP. These changes included a requirement that Treasury make a net present value test available on the internet, based on Treasury's NPV methodology, along with a disclaimer stating that specific servicers' NPV models may differ in some respects.[59] Treasury launched this online NPV calculator in May 2011, and it is available at https://checkmynpv.com/. The law also requires that servicers provide borrowers with certain NPV inputs upon denying the borrowers for HAMP modifications; this differed from Treasury's existing guidance, which required borrowers to ask servicers to see certain NPV inputs within a certain time period if the borrower was denied a modification due to a negative NPV result.

Hardest Hit Fund

On February 19, 2010, the Obama Administration announced that it would make up to a total of $1.5 billion available to the housing finance agencies (HFAs) of five states that had experienced the greatest declines in home prices. This program is known as the Hardest Hit Fund, and several additional rounds of funding have been announced since its inception. The funding comes from the TARP funds that Treasury initially set aside for HAMP. Therefore, all Hardest Hit Fund funding must be used in ways that comply with the Emergency Economic Stabilization Act of 2008 (P.L. 110-343), which means that the funds must be used by eligible financial institutions and must be used for purposes that are allowable under P.L. 110-343.[60]

The five states that received funding in the first round of the Hardest Hit Fund are California, Arizona, Florida, Nevada, and Michigan.[61] The Administration set maximum allocations for each

[58] These changes are described in detail in Treasury's Supplemental Directive 10-02, issued on March 24, 2010, and available at https://www.hmpadmin.com/portal/programs/docs/hamp_servicer/sd1002.pdf.

[59] Servicers are allowed to use their own values for certain NPV inputs on the basis of their own portfolio experience, but such allowed changes are limited and must be approved by Treasury.

[60] Guidelines for HFAs' proposals for the first round of funding are available at http://www.makinghomeaffordable.gov/docs/HFA%20FAQ%20—%20030510%20FINAL%20(Clean).pdf.

[61] See U.S. Department of the Treasury, "Help for the Hardest Hit Housing Markets," press release, February 19, 2010, available at http://makinghomeaffordable.gov/pr_02192010.html. See also "Housing Finance Agency Innovation Fund for the Hardest Hit Housing Markets ("HFA Hardest Hit Fund"): Frequently Asked Questions," available at http://www.makinghomeaffordable.gov/docs/HFA%20FAQ%20—%20030510%20FINAL%20(Clean).pdf, for more information on the program and for maximum funding allocations for each state in the first round.

state based on a formula, and the HFAs of those states were required to submit their plans for the funds to Treasury for approval in order to be awarded funds through the program. The participating states can use the funding for a variety of programs that address foreclosures and are tailored to specific areas, including programs to help unemployed homeowners, programs to help homeowners who owe more than their homes are worth, or programs to address the challenges that second liens pose to mortgage modifications.

On March 29, 2010, the Administration announced a second round of funding for the Hardest Hit Fund. This second round of funding made up to a total of an additional $600 million available to five states that had large proportions of their populations living in areas of economic distress, defined as counties with unemployment rates above 12% in 2009 (the five states that received funding in the first round were not eligible). The five states that received funding through this second round are North Carolina, Ohio, Oregon, Rhode Island, and South Carolina. These states can use the funds to support the same types of programs eligible under the first round of funding, and are subject to the same requirements.[62]

On August 11, 2010, the Administration announced a third round of funding for the Hardest Hit Housing Fund.[63] This third round of funding makes a total of up to $2 billion available to 18 states and the District of Columbia, all of which had unemployment rates higher than the national average over the previous year. Nine of the states that received funds through the third round of funding also received funding in one of the previous two rounds of Hardest Hit Fund funding.[64] The states that received funding in the third round but not in either of the previous two rounds are Alabama, Georgia, Illinois, Indiana, Kentucky, Mississippi, New Jersey, Tennessee, and the District of Columbia. Like the first two rounds of funding, states had to submit plans for the funds for Treasury's approval. Unlike the first two rounds of funding, states have to use funds from the third round specifically for foreclosure prevention programs that target the unemployed.

In September 2010, Treasury announced an additional $3.5 billion of funding to be distributed to the 18 states and the District of Columbia that were receiving funding through earlier rounds, bringing the total amount of funding allocated to the Hardest Hit Fund to $7.6 billion. **Table 3** shows the total maximum allocation of funds, through all rounds of funding, for each state that is receiving funding through the Hardest Hit Fund, along with the amount that has actually been disbursed to each state as of October 2013.[65] (Funds that have been disbursed have been drawn down by states, but may or may not have actually been spent by the states to date. In order to draw down part of its allocation from Treasury, a state may not have more than 5% of its total allocation on hand.) States have until December 31, 2017 to spend their Hardest Hit Fund allocations.

---

[62] See U.S. Department of the Treasury, "Administration Announces Second Round of Assistance for Hardest-Hit Housing Markets," press release, March 29, 2010, available at http://www financialstability.gov/latest/ pr_03292010 html. This press release also includes the maximum funding allocation for each state in the second round.

[63] See U.S. Department of the Treasury, "Obama Administration Announces Additional Support for Targeted Foreclosure-Prevention Programs To Help Homeowners Struggling With Unemployment," press release, August 11, 2010, available at http://financialstability.gov/latest/pr_08112010 html.

[64] Except for Arizona, every state that received funding in one of the first two rounds of the Hardest Hit Fund also received funding in the third round.

[65] Descriptions of the programs that each state is funding through the Hardest Hit Fund are available at http://www financialstability.gov/roadtostability/hardesthitfund html.

Table 3. Hardest Hit Fund Allocations to States

(dollars in millions)

State	Total Funding Allocated	Amount Disbursed as of October 31, 2013	% of Total Allocation Disbursed as of October 31, 2013
Alabama	$162.5	$34.0	21%
Arizona	$267.8	$91.8	34%
California	$1,975.3	$717.5	36%
Florida	$1,057.8	$271.3	26%
Georgia	$339.3	$77.5	23%
Illinois	$445.6	$260.0	58%
Indiana	$221.7	$66.3	30%
Kentucky	$148.9	$64.0	43%
Michigan	$498.6	$146.2	29%
Mississippi	$101.9	$44.3	43%
Nevada	$194.0	$98.8	51%
New Jersey	$300.5	$190.5	63%
North Carolina	$482.8	$270.5	56%
Ohio	$570.4	$239.1	42%
Oregon	$220.0	$155.0	70%
Rhode Island	$79.4	$66.5	84%
South Carolina	$295.4	$112.5	38%
Tennessee	$217.3	$95.3	44%
Washington, DC	$20.7	$14.1	68%
Total	**$7,600.0**	**$3,015.2**	**40%**

Source: Hardest Hit Fund website at http://www.financialstability.gov/roadtostability/hardesthitfund.html and Department of the Treasury, *Troubled Asset Relief Program (TARP) Monthly Report to Congress – October 2013*, http://www.treasury.gov/initiatives/financial-stability/reports/Documents/ October%202013%20Monthly%20Report%20to%20Congress.pdf.

As of the end of October 2013, about $4 billion, or about 40%, of all Hardest Hit Fund funds had been disbursed to states. The percentages of their allocations that individual states have drawn from Treasury range from a low of 21% (Alabama) to a high of 84% (Rhode Island), with most states falling somewhere in between. According to Treasury, there are currently 66 Hardest Hit Fund programs in the 19 states (including DC) that received Hardest Hit Fund allocations, with about 69% of the funding being used for programs targeted to unemployed borrowers.[66]

---

[66] U.S. Department of the Treasury, *Troubled Asset Relief Program (TARP) Monthly Report to Congress – October 2013*, p. 7, http://www.treasury.gov/initiatives/financial-stability/reports/Documents/ October%202013%20Monthly%20Report%20to%20Congress.pdf.

FHA Short Refinance Program

On March 26, 2010, the Administration announced a new Federal Housing Administration (FHA) Short Refinance Program for homeowners who owe more than their homes are worth. Detailed program guidance was released on August 6, 2010.[67] Under the program, certain homeowners who owe more than their homes are worth may be able to refinance into new, FHA-insured mortgages for an amount lower than the home's current value. Specifically, the new mortgage cannot have a loan-to-value ratio of more than 97.75%. The original lender will accept the proceeds of the new loan as payment in full on the original mortgage; the new lender will have FHA insurance on the new loan; and the homeowner will have a first mortgage balance that is below the current value of the home, thereby giving him or her some equity. Homeowners must be current on their mortgages to qualify for this program. Further, the balance on the first mortgage loan must be reduced by at least 10%. This program is voluntary for lenders and borrowers, and borrowers with mortgages already insured by FHA are not eligible.

The FHA Short Refinance Program is similar in structure to the Hope for Homeowners program (described in **Appendix B**), which was still active at the time that the FHA Short Refinance Program began but has since ended. However, there are some key differences between the two programs. First, Hope for Homeowners required that any second liens be extinguished. Under the FHA Short Refinance Program, second liens are specifically allowed to remain in place. Incentives are offered for the second lien-holder to reduce the balance of the second lien, and the homeowner's combined debt on both the first and the second lien is not allowed to exceed 115% of the value of the home after the refinance. Second, under Hope for Homeowners, borrowers could be either current or delinquent on their mortgages and qualify for the program. Under the FHA Short Refinance Program, borrowers must be current on their mortgages. Finally, under Hope for Homeowners, borrowers had to agree to share some of their initial equity in the home with the government when the house was eventually sold. The FHA Short Refinance Program does not appear to require any equity or appreciation sharing.

The FHA Short Refinance Program began on September 7, 2010, and is to be available until December 31, 2014, unless it is terminated before that date.[68] As of January 2013, FHA reported refinancing nearly 2,300 loans through the program.[69] Treasury originally said that it would use up to $8 billion of the TARP funds originally set aside for HAMP to pay for the cost of this program, but has since reduced the total maximum amount that it will spend on the program to just over $1 billion.[70] Any additional program costs would be borne by FHA.

---

[67] FHA Mortgagee Letter 2010-23, "FHA Refinance of Borrowers in Negative Equity Positions," August 6, 2010, available at http://www.hud.gov/offices/adm/hudclips/letters/mortgagee/.

[68] During the 112th Congress, the House of Representatives passed a bill (H.R. 830) which, if enacted, would have terminated the FHA Short Refinance Program and rescinded unexpended funds. Borrowers whose loans had already been refinanced through the program would have been affected if this bill became law. CBO estimated that enacting H.R. 830 would have decreased the federal deficit by $175 million (see Congressional Budget Office, *H.R. 830 FHA Refinance Program Termination Act of 2011*, cost estimate, March 7, 2011, http://cbo.gov/ftpdocs/120xx/doc12089/hr830.pdf). The Senate did not consider the bill.

[69] Federal Housing Administration, *FHA Outlook*, September 2012, p. 4, http://portal hud.gov/hudportal/documents/huddoc?id=ol_current.pdf, and *FHA Outlook*, January 2013, p. 4, http://portal hud.gov/hudportal/documents/huddoc?id=ol0113.pdf.

[70] See U.S. Department of the Treasury, *Troubled Asset Relief Program (TARP) Monthly Report to Congress – April 2013*, pp. 3-4, http://www.treasury.gov/initiatives/financial-stability/reports/Documents/April%202013%20Monthly%20Report%20to%20Congress.pdf.

Other Existing Government Initiatives

A number of additional initiatives or policies have been implemented to attempt to stem the rise in foreclosures and help more homeowners remain in their homes. Although some of these initiatives are now obsolete, many continue to operate. (See **Appendix B** for a description of earlier foreclosure prevention programs that are generally no longer operational.) This section briefly describes certain other recent, ongoing federal programs and policies to prevent foreclosure.

Foreclosure Counseling Funding for NeighborWorks America

Another federal effort to slow the rising number of foreclosures has been to provide additional funding for housing counseling.[71] In particular, Congress has provided funding specifically for foreclosure mitigation counseling to be administered by NeighborWorks America, a non-profit created by Congress in 1978 that has a national network of community partners.[72] NeighborWorks traditionally provides housing counseling to homebuyers and homeowners through its network organizations, and also trains other non-profit housing counseling organizations in foreclosure counseling.

The Consolidated Appropriations Act, 2008 (P.L. 110-161) provided $180 million for NeighborWorks to distribute for foreclosure mitigation counseling, which it has done by setting up the National Foreclosure Mitigation Counseling Program (NFMCP).[73] NeighborWorks competitively awards the funding to qualified housing counseling organizations.[74] Congress directed NeighborWorks to award the funding with a focus on areas with high default and foreclosure rates on subprime mortgages. The Housing and Economic Recovery Act of 2008 (HERA, P.L. 110-289) provided an additional $180 million for NeighborWorks to distribute through the NFMCP, $30 million of which was to be distributed to counseling organizations to provide legal help to homeowners facing delinquency or foreclosure.

Since HERA, Congress has continued to provide funding for the NFMCP through annual appropriations acts, in amounts ranging from $50 million to $80 million. In FY2013, Congress provided $75.8 million for the NFMCP, after taking into account sequestration. **Table 4** shows the funding that has been provided for the NFMCP since its inception.

---

[71] For more information on housing counseling, CRS Report R41351, *Housing Counseling: Background and Federal Role*, by Katie Jones.

[72] Each year, Congress appropriates funding to HUD to distribute to certified housing counseling organizations to undertake various types of housing counseling, including pre-purchase counseling and post-purchase counseling. Congress also appropriates funding to NeighborWorks each year for neighborhood reinvestment activities, including housing counseling. The recent funding provided to NeighborWorks specifically for foreclosure mitigation counseling is separate from both of these other usual appropriations.

[73] For more information on the National Foreclosure Mitigation Counseling Program, see the NeighborWorks website at http://www.nw.org/network/nfmcp/default.asp#info.

[74] HUD-approved housing counseling intermediaries, state housing finance agencies, and NeighborWorks organizations are eligible to receive funds through the NFMCP.

Table 4. Funding for the National Foreclosure Mitigation Counseling Program

$ in millions

Law	Date Enacted	Amount
Consolidated Appropriations Act, 2008 (P.L. 110-161)	December 26, 2007	$180
Housing and Economic Recovery Act of 2008 (P.L. 110-289)	July 30, 2008	$180
Omnibus Appropriations Act, 2009 (P.L. 111-8)	March 11, 2009	$50
Consolidated Appropriations Act, 2010 (P.L. 111-117)	December 16, 2009	$65
Department of Defense and Full-Year Continuing Appropriations Act, 2011 (P.L. 112-10)	April 15, 2011	$65
Consolidated and Continuing Appropriations Act, 2012 (P.L. 112-55)	November 18, 2011	$80
Consolidated and Further Continuing Appropriations Act, 2013 (P.L. 113-6)	March 26, 2013	$76

Source: P.L. 110-161, P.L. 110-289, P.L. 111-8, P.L. 111-117, P.L. 112-10, P.L. 112-55, P.L. 113-6 and the NeighborWorks FY2013 Operating Plan, available at http://www.nw.org/network/aboutUs/policy/documents/FY2013OperatingPlan.pdf.

Notes: The funds appropriated in P.L. 110-289 included funding for legal assistance for homeowners facing foreclosure. Funding for FY2013 takes into account reductions due to sequestration and a 0.2% across-the-board rescission.

Foreclosure Mitigation Efforts Targeted to Servicemembers

The federal government has made a number of efforts to prevent foreclosures specifically among members of the Armed Forces. The Servicemembers Civil Relief Act (P.L. 108-189), which became law on December 19, 2003, prohibits foreclosure completions on properties owned by servicemembers during a period of military service or within 90 days of the servicemember's return from military service.[75] The law also prohibits evictions of active servicemembers or their dependents, subject to certain conditions.

The Housing and Economic Recovery Act of 2008 (HERA, P.L. 110-289) amended the Servicemembers Civil Relief Act to extend the prohibition on foreclosure completions to nine months after a servicemember's return from military service until December 31, 2010. The Helping Heroes Keep Their Homes Act of 2010 (P.L. 111-346) extended the nine-month prohibition on foreclosure completions until December 31, 2012, and the Honoring America's Veterans and Caring for Camp Lejeune Families Act of 2012 (P.L. 112-154) increased the nine-month prohibition to one year and extended it further until December 31, 2014. After that date,

---

[75] This law is a revision of the Soldiers' and Sailors' Civil Relief Act of 1940 (P.L. 76-861), which itself was a revision of the Soldiers' and Sailors' Civil Relief Act of 1918 (P.L. 65-103). Both earlier laws also included foreclosure protections for members of the military on or recently returned from active duty.

the original 90-day period will go back into effect, unless the longer period is again extended by law. HERA also directed the Secretary of Defense to develop a foreclosure counseling program for members of the Armed Forces returning from active duty abroad.

National Mortgage Settlement

In February 2012, 49 state attorneys general and several federal agencies announced a legal settlement with five large mortgage servicers related to concerns regarding their servicing of mortgages.[76] While not strictly a federal foreclosure prevention initiative, the settlement requires the five servicers to provide a minimum dollar amount of foreclosure relief to certain borrowers whose loans are serviced by these institutions.[77] In exchange, the servicers are released from liability for certain civil claims that could otherwise have been raised against the servicers by the participating regulators. Specifically, the five servicers will together provide about $25 billion in aid to borrowers and payments to states and the federal government.[78] The aid to borrowers may take the form of loan modifications, including principal reduction; refinancing for borrowers who owe more than their homes are worth; or payments to certain borrowers whose homes were foreclosed on between 2008 and 2011. The servicers who are subject to the settlement are also required to implement new standards related to how they service mortgages and communicate with borrowers.

For details on the settlement, see http://nationalmortgagesettlement.com/ and CRS Report R42919, *Oversight and Legal Enforcement of the National Mortgage Settlement*, by David H. Carpenter.

Other Foreclosure Prevention Proposals

Some policymakers and others have argued that existing federal foreclosure prevention initiatives have not been effective enough at reducing the foreclosure rate and keeping people in their homes, and that more actions should be taken to assist troubled borrowers. This section briefly outlines some options that have been proposed for further action to help prevent foreclosures.

Changing Bankruptcy Law

One method that has been suggested to help more homeowners remain in their homes is to amend bankruptcy law to allow a judge to order a mortgage loan modification as part of a bankruptcy proceeding. Bankruptcy judges currently have the authority to modify or reduce other types of

---

[76] The five servicers are Ally Financial, Bank of America, Citigroup, JP Morgan Chase, and Wells Fargo. Oklahoma's attorney general did not join the settlement.

[77] The total amount of aid that borrowers receive could be higher than the minimum dollar amount that the servicers are required to provide. This is because servicers receive different amounts of credit towards the amount of relief that they are required to provide depending on the type of borrower aid they offer, based on a complex formula. For example, while servicers receive a dollar of credit for every dollar of some forms of relief that they provide, such as principal reduction, they receive less than a dollar of credit for every dollar of other forms of relief, such as waiving deficiency judgments.

[78] Additional regulatory actions have been brought against these and other mortgage servicers, some of which have also resulted in aid to borrowers. However, the mortgage settlement with the five largest servicers provides the largest dollar amount of borrower assistance.

outstanding debt obligations, including mortgages on second homes and vacation homes, but this authority does not extend to mortgages on primary residences. Opponents of such a change do not want judges to have such broad power to amend a contract after the fact. They argue that allowing these "cramdowns" would make lenders more hesitant to make mortgage loans in the future, since the threat of a loan being modified in this way could make mortgage lending more risky. Supporters of amending bankruptcy law say that, in addition to helping a borrower in bankruptcy avoid foreclosure through a court-mandated loan modification, such a change might also encourage lenders to work with borrowers to modify loans before the bankruptcy process begins in the first place.

During the 111th Congress, provisions to amend bankruptcy law to allow judges to modify mortgages on primary residences were included in H.R. 1106, the Helping Families Save Their Homes Act of 2009, which passed the House on March 5, 2009. However, bankruptcy provisions were not included in the Senate's version of the bill, S. 896, which passed the Senate on May 6, 2009. A modified version of the Senate bill was signed into law (P.L. 111-22) on May 20, 2009, without the cramdown provision. For a description of some of these legislative proposals to amend bankruptcy law to allow judges to order mortgage modifications, see CRS Report RL34301, *The Primary Residence Exception: Legislative Proposals in the 111th Congress to Amend the Bankruptcy Code to Allow the Strip Down of Certain Home Mortgages*, by David H. Carpenter.

In the 112th Congress, bills were introduced to allow judges to modify mortgages on primary residences in bankruptcy under certain circumstances (such as H.R. 4058 and H.R. 1587), but were not reported out of committee. Similar bills (such as H.R. 101) have been introduced in the 113th Congress.

Increased Use of Principal Reduction

Some have called for more widespread use of principal reduction in loan modifications. In mortgage modifications that include principal reduction, some of the principal amount that the borrower owes is forgiven by the lender. Currently, mortgages that are not backed by Fannie Mae or Freddie Mac or government agencies such as the Federal Housing Administration (FHA) are eligible for principal reduction at the discretion of the mortgage holder. Programs such as the HAMP Principal Reduction Alternative, described earlier in this report, provide incentives for reducing principal for certain borrowers. However, the Federal Housing Finance Agency (FHFA), the regulator of Fannie Mae and Freddie Mac, has not allowed principal reduction on mortgages backed by those entities.

The use of principal reduction in modifications has been increasing somewhat, but is only used in about 12% of modifications.[79] Some policymakers and advocates have urged a wider use of principal reduction, and have argued that Fannie Mae and Freddie Mac should be allowed or required to reduce principal on certain mortgages that they own or guarantee. Given that nearly 7

---

[79] Office of the Comptroller of the Currency, *Mortgage Metrics Report Second Quarter 2013*, p. 22, http://www.occ.gov/publications/publications-by-type/other-publications-reports/mortgage-metrics-2013/mortgage-metrics-q2-2013.pdf. According to the OCC, principal reduction was used in 12.1% of mortgage modifications completed in the second quarter of 2013, which represented a decrease in the share of modifications that included principal reduction from the second quarter of 2012, when 15.4% of modifications included principal reduction.

million households with mortgages currently owe more than their homes are worth,[80] advocates of principal reduction argue that it could be an effective tool in preventing foreclosures. Proponents of principal reduction suggest that it might provide an advantage over other types of modifications because it better aligns the amount a borrower owes with the amount that the house is worth, possibly giving borrowers more of an incentive to remain current on the modified mortgage. Advocates also argue that reducing principal can be in the best interest of mortgage holders if the cost of principal reduction is less than the cost of foreclosure. Opponents of more widespread use of principal reduction argue that monthly mortgage payments can be reduced without forgiving mortgage principal, that reducing principal for some borrowers is unfair to others who do not benefit from such relief, and that greater use of principal reduction could encourage some people to default on their mortgages to try to qualify for principal reduction.

For a more detailed discussion of the arguments for and against more widespread use of principal reduction, as well as legislative proposals related to principal reduction from the 112th Congress, see CRS Report R42480, *Reduce, Refinance, and Rent? The Economic Incentives, Risks, and Ramifications of Housing Market Policy Options*, by Sean M. Hoskins.

Issues and Challenges Associated with Preventing Foreclosures

There are several challenges associated with designing successful programs to prevent foreclosures. Some of these challenges are practical and concern issues surrounding the implementation of loan modifications. Other challenges are more conceptual, and are related to questions of fairness and precedent. This section describes some of the most prominent considerations involved in programs to preserve homeownership.

Who Has the Authority to Modify Mortgages?

In recent years, the practice of lenders packaging mortgages into securities and selling them to investors has become more widespread. This practice is known as securitization, and the securities that include the mortgages are known as mortgage-backed securities (MBS). When mortgages are sold through securitization, several players become involved with any individual mortgage loan, including the lender, the servicer, and the investors who hold shares in the MBS. The servicer is usually the organization that has the most contact with the borrower, including receiving monthly payments and initiating any foreclosure proceedings. However, servicers are usually subject to contracts with investors which limit the activities that the servicer can undertake and require it to safeguard the investors' profit. One major question that has faced foreclosure prevention programs, therefore, is who actually has the authority to make a loan modification. Contractual obligations may limit the amount of flexibility that servicers have to modify loans in ways that could arguably yield a lower return for investors. In some cases, loan modifications can result in less of a loss for investors than foreclosure; however, servicers may not want to risk having investors challenge their assessment that a modification is more cost-effective than a foreclosure. This problem can be especially salient in streamlined programs in

---

[80] CoreLogic, *CoreLogic Equity Report, Second Quarter 2013*, p. 2, http://www.corelogic.com/research/negative-equity/corelogic-q2-2013-equity-report.pdf.

which large numbers of loans are modified at once. With such streamlined programs, the cost-effectiveness of loan modifications depends on questions such as how many loans would have likely ended up in foreclosure without the modification, making it more difficult to say whether wholesale loan modifications are in the best interest of investors.

One possible way to partially address the question of who can modify mortgages is to provide a safe harbor for servicers. In general, a safe harbor protects servicers who engage in certain mortgage modifications from lawsuits brought by investors. While proponents of a safe harbor believe that a safe harbor is necessary to encourage servicers to modify more mortgages without fear of legal repercussions, opponents argue that a safe harbor infringes on investors' rights and could even encourage servicers to modify mortgages that are not in trouble if it benefits their own self-interest. The Helping Families Save Their Homes Act of 2009 (P.L. 111-22) provided a safe harbor for servicers who modified mortgages prior to December 31, 2012, in a manner consistent with the Making Home Affordable program guidelines or the since-expired Hope for Homeowners program. The legislation specified that the safe harbor does not protect servicers or individuals from liability for any fraud committed in their handling of the mortgage or the mortgage modification.

Volume of Delinquencies and Foreclosures

Another issue facing loan modification programs is the sheer number of delinquencies and foreclosure proceedings underway. Lenders and servicers have a limited number of employees to reach out to troubled borrowers and find solutions. Contacting borrowers—some of whom may avoid contact with their servicer out of embarrassment or fear—and working out large numbers of individual loan modifications can overwhelm the capacity of the lenders and servicers who are trying to help homeowners avoid foreclosure. Streamlined plans that use a formula to modify all loans that meet certain criteria may make it easier for lenders and servicers to help a greater number of borrowers in a shorter amount of time. However, streamlined plans may be more likely to run into the contractual issues between servicers and investors described above.

Servicer Incentives

Mortgage servicers are the entities that are often primarily responsible for making the decision to modify a mortgage or to begin the foreclosure process. Concerns have been raised that mortgage servicers' compensation structures may provide incentives for them to pursue foreclosure rather than modify loans in certain cases, even if a modification would be in the best interest of the investor as well as the borrower.

Servicers' actions are governed by contracts with mortgage holders or investors that generally require servicers to act in the best interests of the entity on whose behalf they service the mortgages, although, as described above, such contracts may in some cases also include restrictions on servicers' abilities to modify loans. In addition to their contractual obligations, servicers have an incentive to service mortgages in the best interest of investors because that is one way that mortgage servicers ensure that they will attract continued business. However, some have suggested that servicers' compensation structures may provide incentives for servicers to pursue foreclosure even when it is not in the best interest of the investor in the mortgage. For example, servicers' compensation structures may not provide an incentive to put in the extra work that is necessary to modify a mortgage, and servicers may be able to charge more in fees or recoup more expenses through a foreclosure than a modification. Programs such as HAMP provide financial payments to servicers to modify mortgages, but critics argue that these may not be large enough to align servicers' incentives with those of borrowers and investors.[81] The Federal Housing Finance Agency (FHFA) and HUD have announced a joint initiative to consider alternative servicer compensation structures.[82]

For more information on the incentives facing mortgage servicers and previous legislative proposals to implement national mortgage servicing standards, see CRS Report R42041, *National Mortgage Servicing Standards: Legislation in the 112th Congress*, by Sean M. Hoskins.

Possibility of Re-default

Another major challenge associated with loan modification programs is the possibility that a homeowner who receives a modification will nevertheless default on the loan again in the future. This possibility might be of particular concern for lenders or investors if the home's value is falling, because in that case delaying an eventual foreclosure reduces the value that the mortgage holder can recoup through a foreclosure sale. Data released quarterly by the Office of the Comptroller of the Currency (OCC) track the re-default rates of modified mortgages. Data from the second quarter of 2013 show that 17% of loans modified in the first quarter of 2012 were 30 or more days delinquent again three months after the modification, 25% were 30 or more days delinquent six months after the modification, and nearly 31% were 30 or more days delinquent 12 months after the modification. The same data show that a smaller percentage of modified loans were 60 or more days delinquent: 8% of loans were 60 or more days delinquent three months after the modification, 14% were 60 or more days delinquent six months after the modification, and 21% were 60 or more days delinquent 12 months after the modification.[83] Earlier reports from the OCC showed that mortgages modified in earlier quarters tended to have higher re-default rates; the decrease in re-default rates for loans modified in more recent quarters may have to do with an increased focus on modifications that reduce borrowers' monthly payments.

The OCC has begun to include data in its quarterly report that show re-default rates according to whether the loan modification increased monthly payments, decreased monthly payments, or left monthly payments unchanged. The reports include such data for loans modified since the beginning of 2008. The report covering the second quarter of 2013 shows that, for loans modified in 2011, about 15% of loan modifications that resulted in monthly payments being reduced by 20% or more were 60 or more days delinquent twelve months after modification. This compares to a re-default rate of 27% for loans where monthly payments were reduced by between 10% and 20%; 34% for loans where payments were reduced by less than 10%; 17% for loans where payments remained unchanged; and 45% for loans where monthly payments increased. While loan modifications that lower monthly payments do appear to perform better than modifications

---

[81] For one discussion of the economics of mortgage servicing, see Section 3 of the Special Inspector General for the Troubled Asset Relief Program (SIGTARP) Quarterly Report to Congress, October 26, 2010, available at http://www.sigtarp.gov/reports/congress/2010/October2010_Quarterly_Report_to_Congress.pdf.

[82] Federal Housing Finance Agency, "FHFA Announces Joint Initiative to Consider Alternatives for a New Mortgage Servicing Compensation Structure," press release, January 18, 2011, available at http://fhfa.gov/webfiles/19639/Servicing_model11811.pdf.

[83] Office of the Comptroller of the Currency and Office of Thrift Supervision, *OCC and OTS Mortgage Metrics Report: Disclosure of National Bank and Federal Thrift Mortgage Loan Data, Second Quarter 2013*, pp. 31-32, http://www.occ.gov/publications/publications-by-type/other-publications-reports/mortgage-metrics-2013/mortgage-metrics-q2-2013.pdf.

that increase monthly payments, a significant number of modified loans with lower monthly payments still become delinquent again after the loan modification.[84]

The OCC also reports that HAMP modifications appear to perform somewhat better than other types of modifications, possibly because of HAMP's focus on reducing monthly mortgage payments. For example, the OCC reports that about 10% of HAMP modifications completed in the second quarter of 2011 were 60 or more days delinquent six months later, while about 22% of other modifications from the same period were 60 or more days delinquent six months later. For loans modified in the second quarter of 2012, 8% of HAMP modifications were 60 or more days delinquent six months later, compared to nearly 18% of other modifications.[85]

Treasury's own data on the performance of HAMP modifications also show somewhat lower levels of re-default than are seen for other types of mortgage modifications to date. As of September 2013, Treasury reported that 9% of permanent HAMP modifications were 60 or more days delinquent six months after modification, 17% of HAMP modifications were 60 or more days delinquent 12 months after modification, and 30% of HAMP modifications were 60 or more days delinquent two years after the modification.[86]

Distorting Borrower Incentives

Another challenge is that loan modification programs may provide an incentive for borrowers to intentionally miss payments or default on their mortgages in order to qualify for a loan modification that provides more favorable mortgage terms. While many of the programs described above specifically require that a borrower must not have intentionally missed payments on his or her mortgage in order to qualify for the program, it can be difficult to prove a person's intention. Programs that are designed to reach out to distressed borrowers before they miss any payments, as well as those who are already delinquent, may minimize the incentive for homeowners to intentionally fall behind on their mortgages in order to receive help.

Fairness Issues

Opponents of some foreclosure prevention plans argue that it is not fair to help homeowners who have fallen behind on their mortgages while homeowners who have been struggling to stay current receive no help. Others argue that borrowers who got in over their heads, particularly if they intentionally took out mortgages that they knew they could not afford, should face consequences. Supporters of loan modification plans point out that many borrowers go into foreclosure for reasons outside of their control, and that some troubled borrowers may have been victims of deceptive, unfair, or fraudulent lending practices. Furthermore, some argue for foreclosure prevention programs because foreclosures can create problems for other homeowners in the neighborhood by dragging down property values or putting a strain on local governments.

---

[84] Ibid., p. 38.

[85] Ibid., p. 36.

[86] U.S. Department of the Treasury, *Making Home Affordable Program Servicer Performance Report Through September 2013*, p. 7, http://www.treasury.gov/initiatives/financial-stability/reports/Documents/September%202013%20MHA%20Report%20Final.pdf.

To address these concerns about fairness, some loan modification programs reach out to borrowers who are struggling to make payments but are not yet delinquent on their mortgages. Most programs also specifically exclude individuals who provided false information in order to obtain a mortgage.

Precedent

Some opponents of government efforts to provide or encourage loan modifications argue that changing the terms of a contract retroactively sets a troubling precedent for future mortgage lending. These opponents argue that if lenders or investors believe that they could be forced to change the terms of a mortgage in the future, they will be less likely to provide mortgage loans in the first place or will only do so at higher interest rates to counter the perceived increase in the risk of not being repaid in full. Most existing programs attempt to address this concern by limiting the program's scope. Often, these programs apply only to mortgages that originated during a certain time frame, and end at a pre-determined date.

Appendix A. Comparison of Recent Federal Foreclosure Prevention Initiatives

Table A-1. Comparison of Select Federal Foreclosure Prevention Programs

As of November 2013

	Refinancing Programs			Modification Programs	
	Hope for Homeowners (H4H)	FHA Short Refinance Program	Home Affordable Refinance Program (HARP)[a]	Home Affordable Modification Program (HAMP)—Original	HAMP—Principal Reduction Alternative[b]
Program Basics					
Status	Created by P.L. 110-289. Modified by P.L. 111-22.	Obama Administration initiative using authority under P.L. 110-343.[c]	Obama Administration initiative.	Obama Administration initiative using authority under P.L. 110-343.[c]	Obama Administration initiative to modify HAMP.[c]
	Began on October 1, 2008.	Announced March 26, 2010; active since September 7, 2010.	Announced February 2009; active since April 1, 2009.	Announced February 2009; active since March 4, 2009.	Announced March 26, 2010; active since October 1, 2010.
	Ended on September 30, 2011.	Available until December 31, 2014.	Available until December 31, 2015.	Available until December 31, 2015.	Same as HAMP.
	762 loans refinanced through the program.	2,293 loans had refinanced through the program as of January 2013.	2.9 million loans had refinanced through HARP as of August 2013.	59,795 HAMP trial modifications and 909,220 HAMP permanent modifications were active as of September 2013.	14,626 trial PRA modifications and 104,771 permanent PRA modifications were active as of September 2013.[d]

	Refinancing Programs			Modification Programs	
	Hope for Homeowners (H4H)	FHA Short Refinance Program	Home Affordable Refinance Program (HARP)[a]	Home Affordable Modification Program (HAMP)—Original	HAMP—Principal Reduction Alternative[b]
Basic Premise	Allowed certain homeowners who owed more than their homes were worth to refinance into new, FHA-insured mortgages.	Allows certain homeowners who are current on their mortgages, but owe more than their homes are worth, to refinance into new, FHA-insured mortgages.	Allows certain homeowners who are current on their mortgages, but owe over 80% of what their homes are worth, and whose mortgages are owned or guaranteed by Fannie Mae or Freddie Mac, to refinance into new, non-FHA insured mortgages.	Provides financial incentives to servicers and investors to modify borrowers' mortgages so that monthly mortgage payments are no more than 31% of gross monthly income.	Expansion of HAMP to facilitate principal reductions on eligible mortgages.
	Reduced principal balance on first mortgage; maximum loan-to-value (LTV) ratio of new loan depended on borrower's circumstances.	Reduces principal balance on the first mortgage to no more than 97.75% of the home's value. The first mortgage must be reduced by at least 10%.	Does not reduce principal.	Principal reduction is allowed at servicer's discretion, but not required or specifically incentivized.	Requires participating HAMP servicers to consider reducing principal for eligible borrowers who owe over 115% of the value of their home. Provides incentives to lenders/investors specifically for reducing principal.
	Second liens had to be extinguished.	Second liens are allowed to remain; they must be re-subordinated, and total mortgage debt after the refinance may not exceed 115% of the home's value.	Second liens are allowed to remain; they must be re-subordinated.	Second liens are allowed to remain; they must be re-subordinated. The Second Lien Modification Program provides incentives for modification or extinguishment of second liens.	Increases incentive payments available through the HAMP Second Lien Modification Program.

	Refinancing Programs			Modification Programs	
	Hope for Homeowners (H4H)	FHA Short Refinance Program	Home Affordable Refinance Program (HARP)[a]	Home Affordable Modification Program (HAMP)—Original	HAMP—Principal Reduction Alternative[b]
Program Details					
Program Details	Borrower refinanced into FHA-insured mortgage with a lower principal mortgage amount. Original mortgage holder absorbed loss resulting from write-down in mortgage value.	Borrower refinances into FHA-insured mortgage for no more than 97.75% of home's value. Original mortgage holder absorbs loss resulting from write-down in mortgage value.	Borrower can refinance into a new, non-FHA insured loan. The refinanced loan will not reduce the principal balance owed, but it can reduce the interest rate or move the borrower from an adjustable-rate to a fixed-rate mortgage, thereby lowering monthly payments or preventing a payment increase.	Servicers receive incentives to reduce eligible borrowers' mortgage payments to 38% of gross monthly income. Servicer can reduce payments through interest rate reductions, term extensions, and principal forbearance, and may reduce principal at their own discretion. Government shares half the cost of further reducing payments to 31% of monthly income.	Requires servicers who are participating in HAMP to consider principal reduction for borrowers who owe at least 115% of the value of their homes.
	New mortgage amount could not exceed $550,440 (for a one-unit home).	New mortgage amount may not exceed FHA maximum loan limits.	New mortgage, like the original mortgage, cannot exceed Fannie Mae/Freddie Mac conforming loan limits.	The outstanding principal balance on the existing mortgage cannot exceed $729,750 (for a one-unit home). New mortgage balance may be higher due to capitalization of certain allowed fees, such as escrow advances.	Same as HAMP.

	Refinancing Programs			Modification Programs	
	Hope for Homeowners (H4H)	**FHA Short Refinance Program**	**Home Affordable Refinance Program (HARP)[a]**	**Home Affordable Modification Program (HAMP)— Original**	**HAMP— Principal Reduction Alternative[b]**
	New mortgage had to result in a lower monthly mortgage payment than the original loan, but there was no minimum reduction in payment. Maximum loan-to-value ratios and total debt-to-income ratios depended on the borrower's delinquency status and credit score.[e]	New total monthly mortgage payment (including second mortgage payments) must be no higher than approximately 31% of income. New mortgage must result in a reduction of mortgage debt of at least 10% of the amount of the original outstanding principal balance, and must not exceed 97.75% of the home's value. Total household debt may not be more than approximately 50% in most cases.	The new mortgage must benefit the homeowner through a lower interest rate or a more stable mortgage product (for example, a fixed-rate loan instead of an adjustable-rate loan). Borrowers without mortgage insurance (MI) on the original loan are not required to get MI on the new loan.	The new mortgage payment must not exceed 31% of gross monthly income. Borrowers must successfully complete a three-month trial period before the modification becomes permanent.	Same as HAMP. If principal is reduced, the amount of principal reduction will initially be treated as principal forbearance, and then will be forgiven in three equal parts over three years as long as the borrower remains current.
	Borrower paid upfront and annual FHA mortgage insurance premiums.[f] Borrower pays "exit premium" when the home is sold.[g]	Borrower pays upfront and annual FHA mortgage insurance premiums.	If the mortgage already had MI, that MI should be transferred to the new loan.	Mortgages may or may not have MI.	Same as HAMP.

	Refinancing Programs			Modification Programs	
	Hope for Homeowners (H4H)	FHA Short Refinance Program	Home Affordable Refinance Program (HARP)[a]	Home Affordable Modification Program (HAMP)—Original	HAMP—Principal Reduction Alternative[b]
	Second lien-holders had to release their liens.	Allows for existence of a second lien up to a total combined mortgage debt of 115% of home's value. If the second lien is not extinguished, the second lien-holder must agree to re-subordinate the lien.	Second liens are not explicitly addressed.	Second Lien Modification Program provides incentives for the modification or extinguishment of Second Liens.	Second Lien Modification Program still applies; incentives will be increased.
Incentives for Lenders/Servicers/Investors	HUD had authority to provide incentive payments to mortgage servicers and originators of new H4H mortgages.	No incentive payments related to first lien mortgage.	No incentive payments.	Incentives to servicers for making modifications. "Pay-for-success" incentives to borrowers and servicers if borrowers remain current. Incentives to lenders/investors in the form of half the cost of reducing the monthly mortgage payment from 38% to 31% of gross monthly income.	Incentives offered to lenders/investors based on the dollar amount of principal reduced.
	Incentive payments could be made to second lien-holders to facilitate the extinguishment of the lien.	Incentives will be paid to second lien-holders to write down the balance of the second lien.	No incentive payments.	Incentives are offered for second lien-holders to modify or release their liens through the Second Lien Modification Program.	Incentives will be increased for second lien-holders to write down the balance of the second lien.

	Refinancing Programs			Modification Programs	
	Hope for Homeowners (H4H)	FHA Short Refinance Program	Home Affordable Refinance Program (HARP)[a]	Home Affordable Modification Program (HAMP)—Original	HAMP—Principal Reduction Alternative[b]
	Performance of H4H mortgages were not included in certain FHA evaluations of lenders' performance.	Performance of short refinances will not be included in certain FHA evaluations of lenders' performance.	No additional incentives.	Additional incentives are available for investors, borrowers, lenders, and servicers for certain other modification or foreclosure prevention activities.	Additional HAMP incentives continue to apply.
Eligibility Requirements					
Borrower/Mortgage Eligibility Requirements	Borrower could have an FHA-insured or non-FHA-insured mortgage.[h]	Borrower must have a non-FHA-insured mortgage.	Borrower must have a mortgage that is owned or guaranteed by Fannie Mae or Freddie Mac.	Borrower must have a mortgage serviced by a participating servicer.[i]	Same as HAMP.
	Borrower could be current or delinquent on his/her mortgage.	Borrower must be current on his/her mortgage.	Borrower must be current on his/her mortgage.	Borrower may be current (if default is reasonably foreseeable) or delinquent on his/her mortgage.	Same as HAMP.
	Borrower must have experienced a financial hardship.	No hardship requirement.	No hardship requirement.	Borrower must have experienced a financial hardship.	Same as HAMP.

	Refinancing Programs			Modification Programs	
	Hope for Homeowners (H4H)	FHA Short Refinance Program	Home Affordable Refinance Program (HARP)[a]	Home Affordable Modification Program (HAMP)—Original	HAMP—Principal Reduction Alternative[b]
	Borrower's total monthly mortgage payment must have been higher than 31% of gross monthly income. Borrower's net worth could not be greater than $1 million.	No minimum monthly mortgage payment specified.	Borrower owes more than 80% of the value of the home.[j]	Borrower's total monthly mortgage payment must be higher than 31% of gross monthly income. Borrower must not have sufficient liquid assets to make monthly mortgage payments. The unpaid principal balance must be no higher than $729,750 (for a one-unit property). This is the Fannie Mae/Freddie Mac conforming loan limit for high-cost areas.	Same as HAMP. Borrower must owe at least 115% of the value of the home before servicers are required to consider principal reductions.
	Mortgage must have been originated on or before January 1, 2008.	No mortgage origination criteria specified.	Mortgage must have a closing date on or before May 31, 2009.[k]	Mortgage must have been originated on or before January 1, 2009.	Same as HAMP.
	Home must have been the borrower's primary residence.	Home must be the borrower's primary residence.	Home not required to be primary residence.	Home must be the borrower's primary residence or, in some cases, occupied by a tenant.[l]	Same as HAMP.
Property Eligibility Requirements	Property must have been single-family (1-4 unit) home.[m]	Property must be single-family (1-4 unit) home.	Property must be single-family (1-4 unit) home.	Property must be single-family (1-4 unit) home.	Same as HAMP.

	Refinancing Programs			Modification Programs	
	Hope for Homeowners (H4H)	FHA Short Refinance Program	Home Affordable Refinance Program (HARP)[a]	Home Affordable Modification Program (HAMP)—Original	HAMP—Principal Reduction Alternative[b]
Lender/Servicer Participation	Mortgage holders agreed to accept proceeds of new loan as payment in full on the original loan, and FHA-approved lenders agreed to make new H4H loans, on a case-by-case basis.	Mortgage holders agree to accept proceeds of new loan as payment in full on the original loan, and FHA-approved lenders agree to make new FHA-insured loans, on a case-by-case basis.	Fannie Mae- and Freddie Mac-approved lenders are authorized to participate.	Servicers who have signed HAMP participation agreements are required to participate; signing a participation agreement is voluntary.	Servicers who have signed HAMP participation agreements are required to participate in the program changes.

Sources: FHA Mortgagee Letter 2009-43; FHA Mortgage Letter 2010-23; Fact Sheet on FHA Program Adjustments to Support Refinancings for Underwater Homeowners; Fact Sheet on Making Home Affordable Program Enhancements to Offer More Help for Homeowners; FHA Outlook, February 2010; FHFA Foreclosure Prevention and Refinance Report, November 2009/January 2010; Making Home Affordable Program: Servicer Performance Reports; Home Affordable Modification Program Guidelines; HAMP Supplemental Directive 09-01; Fannie Mae and Freddie Mac HARP guidance.

a. Fannie Mae and Freddie Mac have each issued their own specific guidelines for HARP. While these guidelines are generally broadly similar, they differ from one another in some respects.

b. Treasury's detailed guidance on HAMP, including the Principal Reduction Alternative and other related programs, can be found in the Making Home Affordable handbook, available at https://www.hmpadmin.com/portal/index.jsp.

c. While HAMP (and its associated programs) and the FHA Short Refinance Program were created as Obama Administration initiatives, the funding for the program comes from the Troubled Asset Relief Program (TARP). TARP was authorized in P.L. 110-343.

d. An additional 38,283 active HAMP modifications with principal reductions (3,580 active trial modifications and 34,703 active permanent modifications) have been done outside of the PRA.

e. FHA Mortgagee Letter 2009-43. The maximum allowable LTV changed after the program was first created.

f. Using statutory authority provided in P.L. 111-22, HUD reduced the mortgage insurance premiums for H4H from their original levels.

g. Borrowers originally had to agree to share a portion of both their equity in the home and any house price appreciation with HUD when the home was eventually sold. P.L. 111-22 provided the authority to change these requirements. The exit premium is now a payment of a portion of the initial equity in the home after the H4H refinance.

h. FHA Mortgagee Letter 2009-43. When the program first began, only non-FHA-insured loans were eligible.

i. FHA-insured mortgages are eligible for FHA-HAMP, an FHA loss mitigation activity that shares many of the same features as HAMP. VA or USDA mortgages might be eligible for similar programs, subject to the relevant agency's guidance.

j. Originally, HARP allowed homeowners to refinance if they owed up to 105% of the value of their homes. On July 1, 2009, the Federal Housing Finance Agency (FHFA) announced that it would increase the maximum loan-to-value ratio to 125%. In October 2011, FHFA announced that it would remove the LTV cap entirely.

k. Originally, to be eligible for HARP, the original mortgage loan must have been delivered to Fannie Mae or Freddie Mac on or before May 31, 2009. In 2013, the requirement was changed to specify that the closing date on the original mortgage must have been on or before May 31, 2009.

l. Originally, to be eligible for HAMP, the home had to be the borrower's primary residence. Under program changes announced in January 2012, some properties that are occupied by tenants, or that are vacant but which the borrower intends to rent, might qualify for HAMP.

m. FHA Mortgagee Letter 2009-43. When the program first began, only 1-unit properties were eligible.

Appendix B. Recently Ended Foreclosure Prevention Initiatives

In addition to the foreclosure prevention initiatives described earlier in this report, several other foreclosure prevention initiatives were created or announced in recent years but are no longer active. Many of these programs were precursors to the programs that are in place today.

This Appendix describes some of these initiatives, beginning with those that most recently ended. The programs discussed in this Appendix include the Emergency Homeowners Loan Program (which ended September 30, 2011), Hope for Homeowners (which ended September 30, 2011), *FHASecure* (which ended December 31, 2008), Fannie Mae's and Freddie Mac's Streamlined Modification Program, and the FDIC's program for modifying loans that had been held by IndyMac Bank. While these initiatives are no longer active; some borrowers may be continuing to receive assistance through these programs if they began participating in the program prior to the program's end date.

Emergency Homeowners Loan Program

The Dodd-Frank Wall Street Reform and Consumer Protection Act (P.L. 111-203) included up to $1 billion for HUD to use to administer a program to provide short-term loans to certain mortgage borrowers who had experienced a decrease in income due to unemployment, underemployment, or a medical emergency, in order to help them make their mortgage payments. HUD chose to target this funding to the 32 states (and Puerto Rico) that did not receive funding through the Administration's Hardest Hit Fund (described in the "Hardest Hit Fund" section of this report). HUD termed this program the Emergency Homeowners Loan Program (EHLP).[87] By statute, HUD was not able to enter into new loan agreements under EHLP after September 30, 2011.[88]

Table B-1 shows the amounts that HUD designated for the Emergency Homeowners Loan Program for each state that was eligible for funding.

Table B-1. Emergency Homeowners Loan Program Allocations to States

$ in millions

State	Allocation	State	Allocation
Alaska	$3.9	New Hampshire	$12.7
Arkansas	$17.7	New Mexico	$10.7
Colorado	$41.3	New York	$111.6
Connecticut	$32.9	North Dakota	$1.3

[87] Details on the program can be found on HUD's website at http://www.hud.gov/offices/hsg/sfh/hcc/ehlp/ehlphome.cfm.

[88] In the 112th Congress, the House passed H.R. 836, which would have terminated the EHLP and rescinded any unobligated program balances. Any borrowers who had already received loans through the program would not have been affected if the bill had become law. CBO estimated that enacting H.R. 836 would have decreased the federal budget deficit by $840 million. (See Congressional Budget Office, *H.R. 836 Emergency Mortgage Relief Program Termination Act of 2011*, cost estimate, March 7, 2011, http://cbo.gov/ftpdocs/120xx/doc12090/hr836.pdf.)

State	Allocation	State	Allocation
Delaware	$6.0	Oklahoma	$15.6
Hawaii	$6.3	Pennsylvania	$105.8
Idaho	$13.3	Puerto Rico	$14.7
Iowa	$17.4	South Dakota	$2.1
Kansas	$17.7	Texas	$135.4
Louisiana	$16.7	Utah	$16.6
Maine	$10.4	Vermont	$4.8
Maryland	$40.0	Virginia	$46.6
Massachusetts	$61.0	Washington	$56.3
Minnesota	$55.8	West Virginia	$8.3
Missouri	$49.0	Wisconsin	$51.5
Montana	$5.7	Wyoming	$2.3
Nebraska	$8.3		
Total			**$1,000.0**

Source: U.S. Department of Housing and Urban Development, *Obama Administration Announces $1 Billion in Additional Help for Struggling Homeowners in 32 States and Puerto Rico*, press release, October 5, 2010, available at http://portal.hud.gov/portal/page/portal/HUD/press/press_releases_media_advisories/2010/HUDNo.10-225.

The Emergency Homeowners Loan Program was administered through two different approaches. Under the first approach, state housing finance agencies that operate programs that were deemed to be "substantially similar" to the Emergency Homeowners Loan Program could use EHLP funds for their existing programs. On April 1, 2011, HUD announced that it had deemed programs in five states (Connecticut, Delaware, Idaho, Maryland, and Pennsylvania) to be substantially similar to the EHLP and had approved those states' EHLP allocations to be used for their state programs. The EHLP programs in the remaining states used the second approach to administer the program.

Under the second approach, housing counseling organizations that are part of the NeighborWorks network[89] took applications for the program and performed certain other administrative and outreach functions (HUD retained responsibility for program monitoring and compliance, and for managing the note associated with the Emergency Homeowners Loan Program loan). Borrowers were able to begin applying for the program using this approach on June 20, 2011. To apply, borrowers submitted a pre-application to a participating housing counseling agency.[90] After all pre-applications were received, qualified applicants were invited to submit a complete application. If there were more qualified pre-applications than funds available, then borrowers were to be chosen by lottery to submit full applications. Borrowers originally had to submit pre-

[89] NeighborWorks America is a HUD-approved housing counseling intermediary with a nationwide network of housing counseling affiliates. For more information on NeighborWorks in general, see the organization's webpage at http://www.nw.org/network/aboutUs/aboutUs.asp. For more information on NeighborWorks's foreclosure prevention activities, see "Foreclosure Counseling Funding for NeighborWorks America" later in this report.

[90] Information on applying for the EHLP can be found at http://nw.org/network/foreclosure/nfmcp/ehlpconsumers.asp.

applications by July 22, 2011, to be considered for the program, although that deadline was later extended to September 15, 2011.[91]

To qualify for the EHLP, borrowers had to meet certain conditions, including the following:

- Borrowers must have had a household income of 120% or less of area median income prior to the unemployment, underemployment, or medical event that made the household unable to make its mortgage payments;

- Borrowers must have had a current gross income of at least 15% less than the household's income prior to the unemployment, underemployment, or medical event;

- Borrowers must have been at least three months delinquent and have received notification of the lender's intent to foreclose;

- Borrowers must have had a reasonable likelihood of being able to resume making full monthly mortgage payments within two years, and had a total debt-to-income ratio of less than 55%; and

- Borrowers must have resided in the property as a principal residence, and the property must have been a single-family (one- to four-unit) property.

The loans were to be used to pay arrearages on the mortgage as well as to assist the borrower in making mortgage payments for up to 24 months going forward. An individual borrower was eligible to receive up to a maximum of $50,000. Borrowers were required to contribute 31% of their monthly gross income at the time of their application (but in no case less than $25) to monthly payments on the first mortgage, and were required to report any changes in income or employment status while they were receiving assistance. The assistance ends when one of the following events occurs: (1) the maximum loan amount has been reached; (2) the homeowner regains an income level of 85% or more of its income prior to the unemployment or medical event; (3) the homeowner no longer resides in or sells the property or refinances the mortgage; (4) the borrower defaults on his portion of the first mortgage payments; or (5) the borrower fails to report changes in employment status or income.

Loans made through the program were five-year, zero-interest, non-recourse loans secured by junior liens on the property. The loans have declining balances; the borrowers are not required to make payments on the loans for a five-year period as long as the borrowers remain in the properties as their principal residences and stay current on their first mortgage payments. If these conditions are met, the balance of the loan declines by 20% annually until the debt is extinguished at the end of five years. However, the borrower will be responsible for repaying the loan to HUD if one of the following events occurs: (1) the borrower retains ownership of the home but no longer resides in it as a principal residence; (2) the borrower defaults on his or her first mortgage payments; or (3) the borrower receives net proceeds from selling the home or refinancing the mortgage. In the third case, if the proceeds of the sale or refinance are not sufficient to repay the entire remaining balance of the loan, the remaining balance will be considered to have been paid in full and the lien on the property will be released.

---

[91] U.S. Department of Housing and Urban Development, "HUD and NeighborWorks America Accepting Additional Applications for Emergency Homeowners' Loan Program," press release, August 29, 2011, http://portal.hud.gov/hudportal/HUD?src=/press/press_releases_media_advisories/2011/HUDNo.11-177.

To date, HUD has not released final data on how many borrowers participated in the program. Media reports from the time the program ended suggested that between 10,000 and 15,000 borrowers could be assisted, with only about half of the funding allocated to the program ultimately being spent.[92] Participation may have been lower than initially anticipated in part because of delays in getting the program started and borrowers having difficulty meeting the eligibility criteria to qualify for assistance.

Hope for Homeowners

Congress created the Hope for Homeowners (H4H) program in the Housing and Economic Recovery Act of 2008 (P.L. 110-289), which was signed into law on July 30, 2008. The program, which was voluntary on the part of both borrowers and lenders, offered certain borrowers the ability to refinance into new mortgages insured by FHA if their lenders agreed to certain loan modifications. Hope for Homeowners began on October 1, 2008, and ended on September 30, 2011. FHA issued guidance stating that loans had to receive case numbers by July 29, 2011 in order to be eligible for Hope for Homeowners before the program ended.[93]

In order to be eligible for the program, borrowers were required to meet the following requirements:

- The borrower must have had a mortgage that originated on or before January 1, 2008.

- The borrower's mortgage payments must have been more than 31% of gross monthly income.

- The borrower must not have owned another home.

- The borrower must not have intentionally defaulted on his or her mortgage or any other substantial debt within the last five years, and he or she must not have been convicted of fraud during the last ten years under either federal or state law.

- The borrower must not have provided false information to obtain the original mortgage.

Under Hope for Homeowners, the lender agreed to write the mortgage down to a percentage of the home's currently appraised value, and the borrower received a new loan insured by the FHA. The home had to be reappraised by an FHA-approved home appraiser in order to determine its current value, and the lender absorbed whatever loss resulted from the write-down. The new mortgage was a 30-year fixed-rate mortgage with no prepayment penalties, and could not exceed $550,440. Homeowners paid an upfront mortgage insurance premium of 2% of the loan balance and an annual mortgage insurance premium of 0.75% of the loan balance, and any second lien-holders were required to release their liens. When the homeowner sells or refinances the home, he

---

[92] For example, see Joseph De Avila, "Mortgage Aid Effort Falls Short of Its Goal," *Wall Street Journal*, September 29, 2011, http://online.wsj.com/article/SB10001424052970203405504576599110626013214 html and Cara Buckley, "U.S. Mortgage-Aid Program Is Shutting Down, With Up to $500 Million Unspent," *New York Times*, September 28, 2011, http://www nytimes.com/2011/09/29/nyregion/emergency-homeowners-aid-ending-with-up-to-500-million-unspent html.

[93] See FHA Mortgagee Letter 11-20, "Termination of the Hope for Homeowners (H4H) Program," June 10, 2011, http://www hud.gov/offices/adm/hudclips/letters/mortgagee/files/11-20ml.pdf.

or she is required to pay an exit premium to HUD. The exit premium is a percentage of the initial equity the borrower has in the home after the H4H refinance; if the borrower sells or refinances the home during the first year after the H4H refinance, the exit premium is 100% of the initial equity. After five years, the exit premium is 50% of the initial equity.[94]

Under the original terms of the program, the lender was required to write the loan down to 90% of the home's currently appraised value. The upfront and annual mortgage insurance premiums were originally set at 3% and 1.5%, respectively, and second lien-holders were compensated for releasing their liens with a share of any future profit from the home's eventual sale rather than an upfront payment. Furthermore, homeowners were originally required to share a portion of both their equity and any appreciation in the home's value with HUD when the home was eventually sold or refinanced.

On November 19, 2008, HUD announced three changes to Hope for Homeowners in order to simplify the program and encourage participation. The authority to make these changes was granted in the Emergency Economic Stabilization Act of 2008 (P.L. 110-343).[95] These changes did the following: (1) increased the maximum loan-to-value ratio of the new loan to 96.5% of the home's currently appraised value, instead of the original 90%, in order to minimize losses to lenders; (2) allowed lenders to increase the term of the mortgage from 30 to 40 years in order to lower borrowers' monthly payments; and (3) offered an immediate payment to second lien-holders, instead of a share in future profits, in return for their agreement to relinquish the lien.

Congress authorized further changes to the Hope for Homeowners program in the Helping Families Save Their Homes Act of 2009 (P.L. 111-22), which was signed into law by President Obama on May 20, 2009. P.L. 111-22 changed the Hope for Homeowners program by allowing reductions in both the upfront and annual mortgage insurance premiums that borrowers pay; allowing HUD to offer servicers and H4H mortgage originators incentive payments for each loan that was successfully refinanced using Hope for Homeowners; and allowing HUD to reduce its share in any future home price appreciation (and giving HUD the authority to share its stake in the home's future appreciation with the original lender or a second lien-holder). P.L. 111-22 also placed the Hope for Homeowners program under the control of the Secretary of HUD and limited eligibility for the program to homeowners whose net worth did not exceed a certain threshold.

HUD used the authority granted in both of these laws to make changes to H4H from its original form. For example, HUD lowered the mortgage insurance premiums; set the maximum loan-to-value ratio of the new loan at either 96.5% or 90%, based on the borrower's mortgage debt- and total debt-to-income ratios and credit score; offered immediate payments to certain second lien-holders to release their liens; eliminated the shared appreciation feature; and replaced the shared equity feature with the exit premium.[96]

---

[94] See FHA Mortgagee Letter 09-43, available at http://www.hud.gov/offices/adm/hudclips/letters/mortgagee/ 2009ml.cfm. Initially, borrowers had to share a portion of both their equity and any appreciation in the home's value with HUD when the home was sold or refinanced. P.L. 111-22 provided the authority to change this requirement.

[95] The decision to act on the authority granted in P.L. 110-343 and make these changes was ultimately made by the Board of Hope for Homeowners, which included the Secretary of HUD and the Secretary of the Treasury, among others. As described in the text, P.L. 111-22 placed the program under the control of the Secretary of HUD; the Board then took on an advisory role.

[96] For the most recent comprehensive guidance on Hope for Homeowners, including these changes, see FHA Mortgagee Letter 09-43, available at http://www.hud.gov/offices/adm/hudclips/letters/mortgagee/2009ml.cfm.

The Obama Administration issued guidance for servicers on using Hope for Homeowners together with the Making Home Affordable program. This guidance required servicers who are participating in the Making Home Affordable program to screen borrowers for eligibility for Hope for Homeowners and to use that program for qualified borrowers prior to H4H's expiration. The Administration's guidance also offered incentive payments to servicers who used Hope for Homeowners, and to lenders who originated new loans under the program.

The Congressional Budget Office originally estimated that up to 400,000 homeowners could be helped to avoid foreclosure over the life of H4H.[97] In total, about 760 borrowers refinanced through the program.[98] Some have suggested that more borrowers and lenders did not use Hope for Homeowners because the program was too complex. The legislative and administrative changes described above were intended to address some of the obstacles to participating in the program.

FHASecure

FHASecure was a temporary program announced by the Federal Housing Administration (FHA) on August 31, 2007, to allow delinquent borrowers with non-FHA adjustable-rate mortgages (ARMs) to refinance into FHA-insured fixed-rate mortgages.[99] The new mortgage helped borrowers by offering better loan terms that either reduced a borrower's monthly payments or helped a borrower avoid steep payment increases under his or her old loan. *FHASecure* expired on December 31, 2008.

To qualify for *FHASecure*, borrowers originally had to meet the following eligibility criteria:

- The borrower had a non-FHA ARM that had reset.

- The borrower became delinquent on his or her loan due to the reset, and had sufficient income to make monthly payments on the new FHA-insured loan.

- The borrower was current on his or her mortgage prior to the reset. (Some borrowers with a minimum amount of equity in their homes could still be eligible for the program even if they had missed payments prior to the reset.)

- The new loan met standard FHA underwriting criteria and was subject to other standard FHA requirements (including maximum loan-to-value ratios, mortgage limits, and up-front and annual mortgage insurance premiums).

In July 2008, FHA expanded its eligibility criteria for the program, and borrowers had to meet the following revised eligibility requirements:

- The borrower became delinquent on his or her non-FHA ARM because of an interest rate reset or another extenuating circumstance, and had sufficient income to make monthly payments on the new FHA-insured loan.

---

[97] Congressional Budget Office, Cost Estimate, *Federal Housing Finance Regulatory Reform Act of 2008*, June 9, 2008, p. 8, http://www.cbo.gov/ftpdocs/93xx/doc9366/Senate_Housing.pdf.

[98] See Federal Housing Administration, *FHA Outlook*, September 2010 and *FHA Outlook*, September 2011, both available at http://www.hud.gov/offices/hsg/rmra/oe/rpts/ooe/olmenu.cfm.

[99] FHA already offered refinancing options for homeowners who were current on their existing fixed- or adjustable-rate mortgages and continued to do so after the adoption of *FHASecure*.

- The borrower had no more than two payments that were 30 days late, or one payment that was 60 days late, in the 12 months preceding the interest rate reset or other extenuating circumstance.

- If the loan-to-value ratio on the FHA-insured mortgage was no higher than 90%, the borrower may have had no more than three payments that were 30 days late, or one payment that was 90 days late, prior to the interest rate reset or other extenuating circumstance.

- Borrowers with interest-only ARMs or option ARMs must have been delinquent due to an interest rate reset only (and not other extenuating circumstances), and must have been current on their mortgages prior to the reset; the revised eligibility criteria did not apply to these borrowers.

- The new loan met standard FHA underwriting criteria and was subject to other standard FHA requirements (including maximum loan-to-value ratios, mortgage limits, and up-front and annual mortgage insurance premiums).

FHASecure expired on December 31, 2008. In the months before its expiration, some housing policy advocates called for the program to be extended; however, HUD officials contended that continuing the program would be prohibitively expensive, possibly endangering FHA's single-family mortgage insurance program. HUD also pointed to the Hope for Homeowners program as filling the role that *FHASecure* did in helping households avoid foreclosure.[100] Supporters of extending *FHASecure* argued that the statutory requirements of Hope for Homeowners may have offered less flexibility in the face of changing circumstances than *FHASecure*, which could have been more easily amended by HUD.

When *FHASecure* expired at the end of 2008, about 4,000 loans had been refinanced through the program.[101] Critics of the program point to the relatively stringent criteria that borrowers had to meet to qualify for the program as a possible reason that more people did not take advantage of it.

IndyMac Loan Modifications

On July 11, 2008, the Office of Thrift Supervision in the Department of the Treasury closed IndyMac Federal Savings Bank, based in Pasadena, CA, and placed it under the conservatorship of the Federal Deposit Insurance Corporation (FDIC). In August 2008, the FDIC put into place a loan modification program for holders of mortgages either owned or serviced by IndyMac that were seriously delinquent or in danger of default, or on which the borrower was having trouble making payments because of interest rate resets or a change in financial circumstances.

The IndyMac program offered systematic loan modifications to qualified borrowers in financial trouble. The systematic approach means that all loan modifications follow the same basic formula to identify qualified borrowers and reduce their monthly payments in a uniform way. Such an approach is meant to allow more modifications to happen more quickly than if each loan was modified on a case-by-case basis.

---

[100] HUD Mortgagee Letter 08-41, "Termination of *FHASecure*," December 19, 2008, available at http://www.hud.gov/offices/adm/hudclips/letters/mortgagee/2008ml.cfm.

[101] Congressional Budget Office, "The Budget and Economic Outlook: Fiscal Years 2009 to 2019," January 2009, available at http://www.cbo.gov/ftpdocs/99xx/doc9957/01-07-Outlook.pdf.

In order to be eligible for a loan modification, the mortgage must have been for the borrower's primary residence and the borrower had to provide current income information that documented financial hardship. Furthermore, the FDIC conducted a net present value test to evaluate whether the expected future benefit to the FDIC and the mortgage investors from modifying the loan would be greater than the expected future benefit from foreclosure.

If a borrower met the above conditions, the loan would be modified so that he or she had a mortgage debt-to-income (DTI) ratio of 38%. The 38% DTI could be achieved by lowering the interest rate, extending the period of the loan, forbearing a portion of the principal, or a combination of the three. The interest rate would be set at the Freddie Mac survey rate for conforming mortgages, but if necessary it could be lowered for a period of up to five years in order to reach the 38% DTI; after the five-year period, the interest rate would rise by no more than 1% each year until it reached the Freddie Mac survey rate.

FDIC Chairman Sheila Bair estimated that about 13,000 loans were modified under this program while IndyMac was under the FDIC's conservatorship.[102] The FDIC completed a sale of IndyMac to OneWest Bank on March 19, 2009. OneWest agreed to continue to operate the loan modification program subject to the terms of a loss-sharing agreement with the FDIC.[103] Currently, OneWest is a participating servicer in HAMP, described earlier in this report.

Fannie Mae and Freddie Mac Streamlined Modification Plan

On November 11, 2008, James Lockhart, then the director of the Federal Housing Finance Agency (FHFA), which oversees Fannie Mae and Freddie Mac, announced a new Streamlined Modification Program that Fannie, Freddie, and certain private mortgage lenders and servicers planned to undertake.[104] Fannie Mae and Freddie Mac had helped troubled borrowers through individualized loan modifications for some time, but the SMP represented an attempt to formalize the process and set an industry standard. The SMP took effect on December 15, 2008, but has since been replaced by the Home Affordable Modification Program, which was announced in February 2009 and is described in the "Home Affordable Modification Program (HAMP)" section of this report.

In order for borrowers whose mortgages were owned by Fannie Mae or Freddie Mac to be eligible for the SMP, they had to meet the following criteria:

- The mortgage must have originated on or before January 1, 2008.

- The mortgage must have had a loan-to-value ratio of at least 90%.

- The home must have been a single-family residence occupied by the borrower, and it must have been the borrower's primary residence.

---

[102] Remarks by FDIC Chairman Sheila Bair to the National Association of Realtors Midyear Legislative Meeting and Trade Expo, Washington, DC, May 12, 2009. A transcript of these remarks is available at http://www fdic.gov/news/ news/speeches/archives/2009/spmay1209 html.

[103] Federal Deposit Insurance Corporation, "FDIC Closes Sale of IndyMac Federal Bank, Pasadena, California," press release, March 19, 2009, http://www.fdic.gov/news/news/press/2009/pr09042 html.

[104] The private mortgage lenders and servicers who participated in the Streamlined Modification Program were primarily members of the HOPE NOW Alliance, a voluntary alliance of industry members that formed to help homeowners avoid foreclosure. The HOPE NOW Alliance is described in detail in an earlier section of this report.

- The borrower must have missed at least three mortgage payments.

- The borrower must not have filed for bankruptcy.

Mortgages insured or guaranteed by the federal government, such as those guaranteed by FHA, the Veterans' Administration, or the Rural Housing Service, were not eligible for the SMP.

The SMP shared many features of the FDIC's plan to modify troubled mortgages held by IndyMac. Borrowers who qualified for the program had to provide income information that was current within the last 90 days to the mortgage servicer. Based on this updated income information, borrowers' monthly mortgage payments were lowered so that the household's mortgage debt-to-income ratio (DTI) was 38% (not including second lien payments). After borrowers successfully completed a three-month trial period (by making all of the payments at the proposed modified payment amount), the loan modification automatically took effect.

In order to reach the 38% mortgage debt-to-income ratio, servicers were required to follow a specific formula. First, the servicer capitalized late payments and accrued interest (late fees and penalties were waived). If this resulted in a DTI of 38% or less, the modification was complete. If the DTI was higher than 38%, the servicer could extend the term of the loan to up to 40 years from the effective date of the modification. If the DTI was still above 38%, the interest rate could be adjusted to the current market rate or lower, but to no less than 3%. Finally, if the DTI was still above 38% after the first three steps were taken, servicers could offer principal forbearance. The amount of the principal forbearance would not accrue interest and was non-amortizing, but would result in a balloon payment when the loan was paid off or the home was sold.

Negative amortization was not allowed under the SMP, nor were principal forgiveness or principal write-downs. In order to encourage participation in the SMP, Fannie Mae and Freddie Mac paid servicers $800 for each loan modification completed through the program. If the SMP did not produce an affordable payment for the borrower, servicers were to work with borrowers in a customized fashion to try to modify the loan in a way that the homeowner could afford.

Fannie Mae and Freddie Mac completed over 51,000 loan modifications between January 2009 and April 2009, when Fannie and Freddie stopped using the SMP and began participating in the Making Home Affordable program instead.[105] However, it is unclear how many of these loan modifications were done specifically through the SMP.

Federal Reserve Homeownership Preservation Policy

On January 27, 2009, the Federal Reserve announced the Homeownership Preservation Policy.[106] This plan provided guidelines, subject to Section 110 of the Emergency Economic Stabilization Act of 2008 (EESA), to prevent foreclosures on any residential mortgages that the Federal Reserve Banks might come to hold, own, or control, such as mortgage assets that they may receive as collateral for lending to troubled banks.

---

[105] Federal Housing Finance Agency, *Foreclosure Prevention Report: April 2009*, July 15, 2009, available at http://www.fhfa.gov/webfiles/14588/April_Foreclosure_Prevention71509F.pdf.

[106] Details of the Homeownership Preservation Policy can be found on the Federal Reserve's website at http://www.federalreserve.gov/newsevents/press/bcreg/bcreg20090130a1.pdf.

In order to be eligible for a loan modification under the Homeownership Preservation Policy, a borrower would have to be at least 60 days delinquent (although the Fed could make exceptions for households experiencing circumstances that were likely to result in their becoming at least 60 days delinquent). If the expected net present value of a loan modification was greater than the expected net present value of foreclosure, the Federal Reserve Banks could modify mortgages by reducing the interest rate, extending the loan term, offering principal forbearance or principal forgiveness, or changing other loan terms. The modified mortgage would have to have a fixed interest rate, a term of no more than 40 years, and result in a mortgage debt-to-income ratio of no more than 38% for the borrower. The Fed must also have a reasonable expectation that the borrower would be able to repay the modified loan. If the borrower's mortgage debt was greater than 125% of the current estimated value of the property, the Fed would prioritize principal reductions over other types of loan modifications where possible.

This policy applied to whole mortgages that the Federal Reserve Banks held, owned, or controlled. In the case of securitized mortgages in which the Fed had an interest, the Fed would encourage servicers to undertake similar loan modifications and support their efforts to do so.

Author Contact Information

Katie Jones
Analyst in Housing Policy
kmjones@crs.loc.gov, 7-4162